THE CYNIC & THE SOUL

THE QUESTIONS THAT NEED TO BE ASKED

VERONICA CANNING

AND

MOLLY HARVEY

Bloomington, IN   Milton Keynes, UK

authorHOUSE®

AuthorHouse™
1663 Liberty Drive, Suite 200
Bloomington, IN 47403
www.authorhouse.com
Phone: 1-800-839-8640

AuthorHouse™ UK Ltd.
500 Avebury Boulevard
Central Milton Keynes, MK9 2BE
www.authorhouse.co.uk
Phone: 08001974150

First published by AuthorHouse 10/24/2006

ISBN: 1-4259-6822-8 (sc)

Printed in the United States of America
Bloomington, Indiana

This book is printed on acid-free paper.

DEDICATION

This book is dedicated to our husbands and children.

TABLE OF CONTENTS

INTRODUCTION   1

CHAPTER 1:
   CYNIC OR SOUL?   3

CHAPTER 2:
   YOUR LIFE'S PURPOSE   33

CHAPTER 3:
   GET OUT OF YOUR OWN WAY... THE PRESENT   65

CHAPTER 4:
   REVIEW AND RENEW YOUR RELATIONSHIPS   93

CHAPTER 5:
   WHAT LEGACY WILL WE LEAVE?   125

CHAPTER 6:
   CYNIC OR SOUL - SYMBIOSIS OR SABOTAGE   149

INTRODUCTION

Have you ever felt that there was a war going on inside your head between the Cynic and the Soul? Well this book explores this war.

This is an extended conversation between two people with totally different views of the world. It has continued for over three years. It was only recently that we realised that it was actually more than two people talking, that it was an exchange between two different approaches to life: the cynic and the soul.

Veronica, the cynic, is a trained scientist, strategic planner and never believes anything she is told. Molly, the soul, has years of experience of working with people and of seeing beyond the obvious into people's souls. She feels that she gets messages in her meditations, which tell her what to do next.

Many people thought that two women with such different approaches would not get along. The opposite has been the case. This conversation, between seemingly irreconcilable views of life, has been a wonderful journey and a revelation to us both. We wanted to share the results with you, the reader.

As we progressed through our conversation, we found that we had uncovered six main issues, which make up the six chapters in the book. In the conversation, we posed 74 questions and both the cynic and the soul answered each one.

First, we explored the defining issues for a cynic or a soul. Then we looked at the issue of having a life's purpose. Then we progressed beyond having a purpose to seeing what might hold you back from achieving that purpose, how you might get in your own way. The role of relationships in achieving your purpose was discussed and then the whole issue of leaving a legacy was covered. Finally, we looked at the future and our realisation that the cynic and the soul had quite a lot in common.

We hope that you use this book to start a journey of your own. We recommend that you keep a journal of ideas and thoughts as you read through each chapter. We would like you to use our questions and answers to spark your own thoughts. Read both views and then think of your own. We have given you a chart at the end of each chapter for you to mark whether you feel you are leaning towards a cynic or a soul approach.

Ponder your own meaning as you go along. Fill in the chart at the back of each chapter and see if you are more of a cynic or a soul or a mixture of both. Perhaps you may want to query whether each of us has a bit of the soul and the cynic in our make up and whether they might be at war in our heads.

We would be delighted to hear from you if you would like to add any questions as we suspect that this journey has only just begun.

Veronica Canning
Molly Harvey

September 2006

ARE YOU A CYNIC OR A SOUL?
ESTABLISHING THE BASICS

When Molly and I started the process of writing this book we questioned each other on what we each understood by the terms 'soul' and 'cynic'. Imagine the shock we got when we realised what radically different understandings we had. As professional communicators, we have both learnt the hard way how treacherous words can be. My understanding of a word or concept may be different from yours. Our different lives, education, experiences mean we assign different meanings to words and concepts. Often we bring along a lot of baggage as well. So we decided to set out the basics of our understanding of key concepts. You the readers will enjoy the differences and surprising similarities.

CHAPTER 1: CYNIC OR SOUL?

THE QUESTIONS

1. What is soul? 4
2. Where do we find the soul? 6
3. What is cynicism? 8
4. Do we need cynics? 10
5. What is destiny? 12
6. What has destiny got to do with your soul? 14
7. How would I recognise a cynic? 16
8. How does the soul/cynic see the world? 18
9. Do you worry? 20
10. Is there such a thing as soul mates? 22
11. If you have a soul mate can you have a cynic mate? 24
12. How do you listen to your soul? 26
13. Is there a collective unconscious? 28

5 STEPS FOR THE FUTURE 30

ARE YOU A CYNIC OR A SOUL? 31

1. WHAT IS SOUL?

SOUL

Soul to me is our life force; most people think that the soul is in the body. However, I feel the body is in the soul. Our soul reaches out further than the body. We can sense the soul physically from the time we are in the womb and it leaves when we take our last breath. The soul is eternal: it has no beginning and no ending, and it is a subtle entity that cannot be measured by any physical process or instrumentation. As an energy, the soul has within itself qualities that are both masculine and feminine. Soul is that inner part of light that shines out from each and every human being and we make that connection when we look into another human being's eyes.

"When you learn to be you, set your soul free."

CYNIC

I often hear people say, "oh, that person has a soul" or as my dad used to say when my daughter was young, "her soul has been here before". She used to say this when she came out with something quite profound as only a four-year-old child can. My dad believed that people had a soul and I wondered if he meant that some people have old souls – and that we see them when they appear in the wisdom of some very young children.

This made me wonder about what a soul might be. Is it something inside us or all around us?

Is it our mind, our subconscious or is it energy? Do we all belong to one big energy system and is our soul our portion of that energy system?

If our soul was energy it would move through time and space and not die. Perhaps a young person's soul can be glimpsed in the seemingly old wisdom they give us.

I believe that our souls are where the inner deep, wise, real person exists. We all have souls but not many of us ever make meaningful contact with our own. It requires stillness, thoughtfulness to make the time, space and conditions conducive to finding your soul and to connect to it.

Paradoxically – you never miss your soul when you fill your life with hyperactivity. If you are lucky to find it – you must hang onto that connection to soul and never let it go again.

"Be still and seek out a connection with your soul."

2. WHERE DO WE FIND THE SOUL?

SOUL

In many human beings it is wrapped away like a jewel waiting to be re-awakened. It hasn't gone anywhere; it's just that in this 21st century many humans become slaves to ego, lust, attachments and materialism. We are sometimes sucked into these negative influences. That's very often when people begin to search for peace and happiness, which are some of the qualities of the soul. Sometimes we even get caught up looking for the soul on the outside and go through numerous broken relationships looking for our soul in others, when if only we stopped for a moment and took time to be silent, we could re-connect with that beautiful part of light that lives within us.

In the late 1980s I lived in London for about two years. I got caught up thinking bigger was better, working myself to exhaustion. One night I was travelling home on the Tube, when I opened my bag and took out my pay cheque which was £6000 for my month's work. In the 1980s that was a lot of money, yet here I was getting home late again. Looking at this piece of paper I felt so exhausted, so empty, so tired. In that moment I made a decision that bigger wasn't better. I wanted to find my soul again. I had become caught up in hurry-sickness, wrapping my soul away and was like a robot on autopilot each day.

"Learn to stay centred in your day by staying in touch with the living flame inside of you."

CYNIC

I spent most of my working life until 1997 working at full tilt, always busy focussing on the next challenge, rarely celebrating the present victories and successes. I am not alone in this kind of behaviour. We are all changing and becoming more success focussed. Material possessions, house, car, designer clothes, or jewellery are increasingly measuring our success. Forget that you can drive only one car at a time; now the 'truly' successful have stables of cars. Most are so valuable that they are afraid to put them on the road!

If you go down this road without thinking, if you have no time to question your path in life or how you are living it, then you may never connect with your soul. Why? Simply because you haven't even realised it is there, so if you don't know about it you will not go looking for it.

Some people are blessed in that they make wise decisions early in life and connect with their souls early. They are the rare ones. Increasingly, the rush is to merely possess.

Will this change? Not for a long while. The soul has come to inhabit the fringes of our society's consciousness.

"Don't think acquiring lots of possessions equals success."

3. WHAT IS CYNICISM?

SOUL

A great question: to me, cynicism is our ego telling us not to go forward. At the end of the day most human beings long for peacefulness, yet so often we get caught up in the turmoil and go in the opposite direction. I have watched many friends throughout my life have some great ideas thrown away because of cynicism. When we let the cynic side of our personality take over, we tend to get caught up in arguing and confronting people. Life becomes a power struggle, suddenly we need to compete and compare ourselves to others. Cynics also secretly worry a lot and when our inner world is focussed more on worry, we have less time to be peaceful. The cynic in us also chatters to us all day. For example, it will tell us to forget that meditation stuff and tell us to keep busy, keep pushing. The more you let the cynic chatter go on in your head, the less space you will have for peace and learning in your life.

"Transformation will come when you let go of your attachments."

CYNIC

Clearly, it means different things depending on your view of the world. For me, cynicism should be the under layer of every decision you make. I don't believe in taking everything at face value and trusting in everything and everyone. I like to look beneath the surface and see what is really there. I feel I need a deeper understanding of the issues before I can make a decision.

If you trust in your destiny and a higher guiding force and put yourself in the hands of that force, you will dislike people who ask lots of questions. People like me, questioning cynics. I had a scientific training and so have a questioning mind. I simply don't believe everything I am told, I need proof. If you are not of this mindset and don't feel the need to question everything then you can find a questioning approach unwelcome and reach for the label 'cynical'!

Cynicism is the antidote to blind optimism and has a place in creating a balanced outlook on life. Molly and I are opposites on this. Molly believes if she buys and drinks green grasses she will be healthier and thinner. I automatically want to see the product details, profit margin and scientific proof. She believes it will work. I think at best it's unscientific; at worst it's daft!

"A dose of cynicism is a very useful tool to apply to every decision in your life."

4. Do We Need Cynics?

Soul

Yes and no. A certain amount of cynicism can be healthy and many new ideas and different paths have been opened up due to looking and seeing the world or a challenge in different ways. As I said earlier, cynicism to me is our ego and our ego is what motivates us to get up in the morning, to go out and do something with our life. Many times in my life I have shared an idea with someone and they tell me all the reasons why I should not do it and then get cynical about it. I listen and hear all that is said, then go away by myself and meditate. I go to that quiet and inner place, that point of light where my own ego does not live. Very often, the person has done me a great favour as I have thought the process through in a different way and I do it anyway. However, I have seen other people's self esteem destroyed because of the cynical thoughts of others. In this 21st century, we need to be more mindful about what language we use and thoughts we share and tell others about them. Thoughts are things and if you are very negative about something, the person who receives your negative feedback could carry it for a long time.

As a child, I can recall my mum making comments, always in small ways, such as, "You're a dunce" or "Your grades at school are never as good as your cousin's". It has taken me many years to delete those comments from my mind. I am also sure that when she said those words she never thought I would take them so personally. She was doing the best she knew at the time.

So my thoughts on cynics are, if you can choose to give positive rather than negative feedback, always go for the positive. Balance is the key.

"Everything that is in the entire universe is connected to being in the flow."

CYNIC

We need cynics because they have a key role in questioning and deepening our understanding of the world. Driven visionaries and mould breakers are vital to the continued evolution of our society and our business world. They tend to push forward through all the barriers. They don't question, they move. However, when it comes to implementation the cynics are often the ones who make it happen. Through questioning they improve the idea and make it practical.

This form of cynicism is open and questioning-looking for the meaning, the insights, the undiscovered. This is useful cynicism. The opposite can be quite destructive. This is the naysayer! The person who is intrinsically negative: "We can't do that, it's never been done before" or, "It's more then my job's worth" are their favourite phrases. These negative people are afraid of shining brightly or afraid to take a decision. They are a force of negativity but they give cynics a bad name. They are not cynics, they are psychic vampires.

Molly is wholly optimistic and finds answers in meditation. I prefer the 360 degree questioning approach. Someday I will persuade Molly to take a spreadsheet to her meditation.

"Constructive questioning before you leap is never a bad thing."

5. WHAT IS DESTINY?

SOUL

Destiny is something with which we are born. I passionately believe each human being has a purpose in this world. Wasn't Mozart destined to create great music? Mother Theresa destined to be a light to the poor and touch so many lives? Since I was a small child I have always felt an invisible presence guiding me towards my destiny. Some people become seekers and search for their destiny, whilst others let destiny find them. I also believe that we get choices along the way as to how we carry out our lives.

William James, a psychologist and philosopher, once wrote:

> "In the dim background of our mind we know meanwhile what we ought to be doing... But somehow we cannot start... Every moment we expect the spell to break... but it does continue pulse after pulse, and we float with it..."

I have come to the same conclusion as William James; that somewhere deep, deep inside all of us is our purpose, what we are destined to do and be and I don't believe anybody's destiny is grander or better than anyone else's – it just is.

"Learn to get in touch with the timeless presence that lives inside of you."

CYNIC

Is destiny predetermined or do we create our own? Is destiny the same as purpose? Is your life's destiny your life's purpose? These questions come to mean more as you get older. At different milestones in your life you pause and reflect on why you are here, what you have done and what you will do with the balance of your life.

At the beginning of your life you look forward and think of your future goals. At mid stage you look forward and back and this can precipitate a crisis! The midlife crisis. People often ask, "Is this as good as it gets?" or "Is this my life?". This can lead to a complete turnaround-divorce, changing careers, adopting children, starting a new business, emigration. Towards the end of your life you look back and reflect and plan for the final goals before you go.

Where does destiny fit into this view? If you feel that you came with a predetermined destiny then your biggest challenge may be finding it before it's too late. I firmly believe that God helps them that help themselves. I could not trust completely to a life where I felt my destiny was preordained and where my mantra was "What will happen will happen – my destiny will triumph".

I believe you make your own destiny. You came here on earth with a set of gifts, talents and abilities. Your environment affects you and you grow up and go out into the world. You make decisions every minute of every day and every decision affects your destiny. Your destiny is like a chameleon, it changes with every decision.

This is why so many self-help books from Jack Canfield to Stephen Corey emphasise the importance of life's vision because they know the importance of every decision. You can make you own destiny by setting out a crystal clear realisation for yourself and making every decision a step in that direction. Molly believes that we come on earth with a purpose, a destiny. I believe we arrive and get out our filofaxes and make our destiny.

"Every decision you make shapes your destiny."

6. WHAT HAS DESTINY GOT TO DO WITH YOUR SOUL?

SOUL

Destiny is our purpose. It is why we are here. Our soul is that illuminated spark that exists within us. It is an inside-out process instead of an outside-in one. When we follow our destiny from our soul's calling, our lives unfold like a lotus flower. When we follow our destiny from our ego we run around in circles getting nowhere. The ego keeps us from being free. When destiny and soul interlink we live at an altered state and trust in the flow of life. From an early age of growing up in Co. Waterford I felt a strong sense of purpose. It was as if I was destined to speak to large numbers of people all over the world. Often, when I was bored in history classes, I would go to that quiet place inside and daydream about what I would do when I grew up. Now I realise that during those times I was already being prepared for the work that is unfolding in my life now. Over the years I have sometimes tried to follow my destiny from my ego and I have always ended up tired, frustrated and empty. Destiny has helped me realise that we are more than just this body; we are souls within a body.

Rumi once said:

> "You were born with
> Potential
> You were born with
> Greatness
> You were born with
> Wings
> Learn to use them and Fly

"The silent witness is the source of all synchronicities in our lives."

CYNIC

Destiny has everything to do with your soul. However, I don't agree with the optimistic view that destiny and soul are always linked and linked for the greater good. Sadly, I feel that both can elude your conscious mind and so exist outside of your present knowledge. I believe that you need to find both in your life; you need to find your soul and know it. I believe that you need to make your destiny and, if you are lucky, you align the two. I have seen too many lost people who see no purpose to their life and feel no depth or meaning in the actual living of their everyday life to easily accept that you easily find or connect the two.

You are exceptionally lucky if you find a purpose for your life early enough with the discovery of your soul. You can achieve great things. More usually, the discovery of destiny and soul can come after a great shock or sadness, which rocks you to the core. The sudden death of a loved one, the fright of serious illness or huge financial loss can trigger deep searching. It is a pity that so many of us have to be shocked into searching for our soul, our lifes' purpose and destiny. Would it not be wiser to start the search earlier?

Molly feels she has had a sense of her destiny from an early age and is resolute in this. I feel my soul has a hard time getting out but life experience has meant its time has now come. However, I prefer to hang onto the freedom to constantly tinker with my life's purpose and destiny.

"Connecting your destiny to your soul is a lifelong process."

7. HOW WOULD I RECOGNISE A CYNIC?

SOUL

To me a cynic is the person who seems to know the price of everything and the value of nothing. They get so consumed in the finer detail of life that they sometimes become blinkered and short sighted. Life can pass them by and then they will moan about that too. Cynics seem to self-sabotage themselves and life is sometimes so very hard on them. Life can be so complicated, always expecting to fail and sometimes achieving great power when things don't work out. Very often their comment to you will be, "See, I told you so and so wouldn't listen". Cynics can also be very quick witted and funny and with this in mind I will end with this sentence. I asked a friend, Jim Robertson, how he viewed the cynic and his reply was, "The cynic is someone who wins an Oscar for sneering without much effort".

"Obstacles are a part of life, stop and let go."

CYNIC

Easily, the raised eyebrow, the questioning look, the set of questions, the pause before action. Molly would say, "it's 'the look'." When she tells me that spirits are in the room and that they are guiding me, she knows from the look on my face that I am having a serious cynic moment.

Of course, you can spot a fully paid up member of the negative club a mile away. But don't be confused, they are not genuine cynics, they are just frightened negatives.

Instead, they look for the questioner, the seeker, the puzzler, the deep seeker or the beneath- the-surface person. Here you will find the real cynic and if you give them the space and time you will get insights. Asking good questions is a rare gift and a good cynic has a gift for this. An instinct that prompts them to ask just the right questions. When you find a cynic at work in his or her own area of expertise, expect real insights. They will track down the deeper meaning, even if it drives all the soul people mad.

Molly makes her mind up and follows her soul's direction. She finds deep meanings and guidance in her meditations. Then she finds me waiting with the questions. It's wonderful when she goes back to the meditation for answers to these questions, true synergy.

"Cultivate a questioning approach and develop your insightful thinking."

8. HOW DOES THE SOUL/CYNIC SEE THE WORLD?

SOUL

The soul sees the world through the eyes of oneness. The soul has the ability to see past what isn't happening to what is. In the soul's world, time and space are illusions, the soul is timeless. The soul sees and hears the resonance pattern of the world, it understands that everything is energy. The soul in each of us is the extension and the love of God. To the soul there is no separation, only connections.

It is man's ego that creates war on this planet. When we connect with another human being and look deeply into their eyes, we make a soul connection and realise we are all divine light. The light that I have, you have. Our souls are the God spark that lives within each and every one of us. The soul has no need to try and control and push, it knows that everything unfolds as it is meant to.

When we allow our souls to be, we release our true selves and realise that our beingness is enough.

"Every moment you live you have a choice to be at peace or be at war."

CYNIC

The cynic sees the world clearly, vividly and deeply. The cynic sees the dangers, the opportunities, and the challenges. The cynic sees all the sides, the positives and the negatives, and unfortunately sees them all at the same time. This can be a mixed blessing. Really soulful people who feel they are living a destiny have the great gift of going steadily forward. They bask in the glow of the rightness of destiny, often refusing to see the negatives. I feel this is mainly because they don't look for them. I staunchly defend the wisdom of seeing the pros and cons. Cynics see the negatives and that is their greatest challenge, to see beyond the negatives and to find balance. The downfall of the cynic is when they go into the negatives too much, sometimes even taking up residence in negativity.

Molly sees the possible in everything and is extremely positive; it's just as well for the world that she has a cynical companion on her journey.

*"Look at the world with open eyes, see the negative
and the positive in everything."*

9. DO YOU WORRY?

SOUL

The soul does not worry. It lives from a world of abundance not scarcity. People who spend most of their lives worrying are not happy; in fact they are usually miserable. Worry is a choice. You can keep on moaning and worrying or do something about it. The sad thing in life is some people secretly enjoy worrying, it becomes a habit and if they didn't have anything to worry about they would have to find something. It can also be a great way of getting attention from other people. When we worry we cut off abundance. I remember many years ago hearing a quote, "Worry is the interest not yet due on your bank account."

As human beings we have a choice, to live a life of worry or a life of intention. When we worry we plant weeds and energy zappers in the garden of our minds. When we live from intention we plant beautiful flowers, daffodils, bluebells and tulips. Worry is like woodworm, it can eat your mind away. The soul sees worry as wasted energy. I believe we reap what we sow. Take responsibility and sow happiness and joy instead of fear and doubt, which is the realm of worry.

"When struggling in life and you feel you are not in the flow, hand over your problems to the universe and wait."

CYNIC

Not as much now as I get older but I have worried for Ireland in my time. I tend to start with the worst case scenario and work back from that to the present. Once I have decided on my plan to cope with the worst scenario I can calm down as I have faced the worst. This is a gut reaction! The need to hope for the best and prepare for the worst.

I understand that a soulful person like Molly sees the right way to their destiny. She relies on signs, omens, mirages, intuitions, and finally synchronicity. She flows along a path being guided by external forces like nature, love, and the rightness of things. She trusts a lot, appears not to question the messages and signs but believes that she will be shown the way.

I have another friend who believes that God will direct her every step of the way through life. She asks for guidance on every decision and accepts it gracefully. She seems to live a peaceful and content life despite having suffered some major setbacks, but has used her soulful approach to weather them. It is her trust in the guiding hand of a greater power that sustains her. I can see what a wonderful gift this can be for a soulful person.

However, as a cynic I would still need to keep some control over my destiny. I want to determine the directions of my life and would have difficulty accepting total guidance from outside of myself. I would always need to worry about potential problems and make a contingency plan or two.

"A life without worry is a myth. It's always better to build contingency plans to get you through"

10. Is there such a thing as soul mates?

Soul

From the beginning of time, man and woman got together for procreation; most people in life look for a soul mate. We as human beings have an intense need to be loved. However, I think we can have different kinds of soul mates: some people come into our lives as teachers and we learn from them while others come in as anàm caràs (soul friends) and we have a lot in common with them, our soul dances when they are around. Then there is that person out there most of us think is a soul mate, who is out there searching for us as we are for them. Soul mates enter our lives for a reason, a season or a lifetime.

A friend of mine was distraught recently when their marriage had ended and was quite bitter about the break up. One day, whilst having a coffee, I said to her, "Can you see the blessings of your last relationship?" She replied, "No" to which I said, "What about the two beautiful children you both brought into the world?" Eighteen months later she now has a relationship she always dreamed of, so if her marriage had not ended when it did, maybe she would never have known the happiness she has now found.

Sometimes in life, we have to let go of the old to find something even more special in life.

"Everyone we meet in life is a teacher.
We meet them for a reason, a season or a life time."

CYNIC

Soul mates come to you on your journey through life but experience has taught me to be wary of whom you allow to become close to you. Not everyone who professes to be your soul mate is genuine; frequently they merely look like soul mates.

I reckon you are lucky if you meet more than a half dozen soul mates that stay with you throughout your life. If you close your eyes and think of the people you would be totally honest with and share your innermost thoughts you will see the faces of your soul mates.

It's important to realise some people will go part of the journey with you but while they are close friends they are not soul mates.

You discover your real soul mate when you know someone accepts you for who you are not what you do or own. When someone stays your friend after they have seen the worst of you then you know you have found a soul mate.

"Learn how to distinguish the real soul mate from all the pretenders and you will have found a precious jewel"

11. IF YOU HAVE A SOUL MATE CAN YOU HAVE A CYNIC MATE?

SOUL

Interesting question and the answer is yes, you can. I know many friends where one of them views their life from their soul's viewpoint and their partners view life from the cynic's eyes. At times, their relationship can go through very turbulent times because the energy can be push-pull. The cynic always sees the reasons why you should not go forward; the soul doesn't see the down side.

I recently had a friend who called me up for advice. She had been married for forty years to her husband and she felt he had clipped her wings all her life. She had given in to his demands and advice. Her soul was tired and she felt trapped as if she was a lion in a cage. I encouraged her to sit down with her husband and explain how she felt and that she needed to follow what her soul was telling her. The outcome was her husband said he never realised she felt that way and would support her in future.

"If you think the world is an unusual place to be, that is what it will be."

CYNIC

I believe that you can have a cynic mate as well as a soul mate.

A soul mate accompanies you through the highs and lows of life. They are there for you through everything. I feel a cynic mate can also accompany you but in their own unique way. I feel every soulful person should have a cynic in their lives to give them balance otherwise they will think everything happens for a reason. They will miss the fun of questioning everyone's motives and seeing the bad in people!

The cynic mate will question your assumptions, your ideas and your complacency. They will offer insights. They will always give you a deeper insight. Sometimes in your life, you have more need of insight than blind faith and support.

A friend of mine was contemplating a radical career change and we talked deeply about it. I gave her the cynic's view and equipped her with a number of probing questions. She reviewed the whole situation with this new insight. She finally decided to turn down the job offer and persue another career.

"Add spice to your life go find a cynic mate"

12. How do you listen to your soul?

SOUL

Humans listen to their soul in many different ways. To me personally, I go into silence and I hear that beautiful voice inside of me. It is never judgemental or angry, it just is. When I hear it or feel it, it fills me with awe and grace. When we listen to our soul it guides us gently to the next step in our lives.

A few years ago, I was standing in a queue at the shop in the Findhorn Foundation. There was a gentleman in front of me who had a packet of biscuits in his hand and was searching for his money to pay. People were tut tutting in the queue. He said to the assistant, "I can't find my money, I'll have to leave them." I felt my soul quietly say to me, *pay for them*, so I paid for the biscuits and ran out after the man. I handed him the biscuits and at first he looked shocked. I smiled and walked away. My soul danced all the way back to the caravan I was staying at. Let your soul guide you.

"To listen to your soul's message you have to slow down and tune in."

CYNIC

We all hear our souls but some of us listen better than others.

A thinking, questioning person, would need to understand what was going on. They would need to have a rational explanation. So listening to your soul for a person like that presumes they know that they have a soul and secondly that it talks. Molly's influence has opened this up to me and re-echoes the wisdom my parents tried to give me. They saw it as trusting to God who would guide you.

I have an alternative explanation for Molly's talking soul. I often give presentations on what I call AHA thinking. The process involved could be the soul talking, I'm not sure.

I recommend that you use this process when you face a problem which is complex and seemingly insoluble. You first state the problem clearly and specifically. Then you examine it from a variety of angles, especially trying to think outside your particular box. In effect, you bombard your brain to make it think laterally. Then in the next phase, you leave the problem and the new ideas, no matter how mad, to rest in your subconscious. It's a good idea to sleep on the problem.

Your subconscious mind works away on problems whilst we are asleep and then unexpectantly throws up the answer. We have what is called a cognitive snap. We experience it as a sudden AHA moment when the answer appears.

I wonder if this might be Molly's soul calling, especially as the insights of meditation frequently come at dawn when the mind starts working.

*"Find the time to think creatively and to access
the riches in your own head."*

13. IS THERE A COLLECTIVE UNCONSCIOUS?

SOUL

We are all connected by the power of intention. The invisible presence that flows through me also flows through you and everyone else on this planet. Have you never experienced synchronicity, where you thought of something or someone and within hours or days it unfolded. I recommend you read *The Field* by Lynne MacTaggert. Her book is filled with studies supporting the existence of a higher energy division or collective unconscious. Dr Wayne Dwyer shares a lovely story by Chuang Tzu in his book, *The Power of Intention*.

There once was a one-legged dragon called Hui. "How on earth do you manage those legs," he asked a centipede, I can hardly manage one!" "Matter of fact," said the centipede, "I do not manage my legs."

There is something invisible and bigger that manages us all. To me that is the collective unconscious.

Once we make a conscious connection between our physical personality and the collective unconscious, we can then get on with the reason why we were born into this life, here, this time.

"We are all one. We are all interconnected."

CYNIC

Reading the words of Carl Jung, who first described the collective unconscious, has convinced me that indeed there is a deeper level than the individual subconscious. As a biologist I can accept that each person passes on their DNA to their offspring so why not also that portion of the unknown, called the collective unconscious. It would explain a lot about how national cultures survive despite profound attack, like the North American Indians, about the sacredness of certain places, the evil of others.

If we think of it as inheriting a reservoir of latent images from our ancestral past which includes all our ancestors then we can inherit predispositions for experiencing and responding to the world in ways that our fathers and mothers did. Consider the irrational fear of snakes, especially in Ireland, where there are none. All banished by Saint Patrick! This predisposition to fear may have come from the collective unconscious.

I feel this may often appear as the souls who visit with Molly on a regular basis.

"Our ancestors can pass on their wisdom to us"

5 STEPS FOR THE FUTURE

Five steps on how to live from the soul:

1. Take time each day to meditate

2. Get out of your own way

3. Learn to be a human being instead of a human doing

4. Hand over your worries to God

5. Live each day from the mindset of abundance not scarcity

Five steps on how to live from the cynic:

1. Learn how to ask good questions

2. Develop an insightful approach, always go beyond the obvious

3. Every decision you make shapes your destiny so make thoughtful ones

4. Study and learn creative thinking techniques

5. Make time to think creatively every day and access the riches in your own head

ARE YOU A CYNIC OR A SOUL?

THE QUESTIONS	CYNIC	SOUL
1. What is soul?		
2. Where do we find the soul?		
3. What is cynicism?		
4. Do we need cynics?		
5. What is destiny?		
6. What has destiny got to do with your soul?		
7. How would I recognise a cynic?		
8. How does the cynic/soul see the world?		
9. Do you worry?		
10. Is there such a thing as soul mates?		
11. If you can have a soul mate can you have a cynic mate?		
12. How do you listen to your soul?		
13. Is there a collective unconscious?		
SUBTOTAL		

CHAPTER 2: YOUR LIFE'S PURPOSE

THE QUESTIONS

1. What does life purpose mean to a cynic/soul?   34
2. Does everyone's soul have a purpose?   36
3. How do you find your purpose?   38
4. Does everyone have a destiny?   40
5. What is difference between destiny and fate?   42
6. How do you know you are on purpose?   44
7. How big can your purpose be?   46
8. Do begrudgers have a role?   48
9. If you don't take responsibility
   for your life, what happens?   50
10. Is a questioning approach good?   52
11. How do you know you are on your path?
    How do you get in touch with your soul's path?   54
12. Does anyone ever die without
    figuring out their soul's path?   56
13. Do we have intuition? Can we trust our intuition?   58
14. What is happiness?   60

5 STEPS ON HOW TO GET IN
   TOUCH WITH YOUR LIFE'S PURPOSE   62

ARE YOU A CYNIC OR A SOUL?   63

1. WHAT DOES LIFE PURPOSE MEAN TO A CYNIC/SOUL?

SOUL

We are born into the world each with a unique life purpose. It is planted inside of us. Some people know from an early age why and what they are here to do whilst others go searching; I call it the wilderness years. We are out there looking for our purpose when in fact it is inside of us at all times. To the soul, life purpose means to give away, be of service to others. When you learn to be of service to others you will learn what your life purpose is and your soul will dance.

From a very early age I felt I was here for a purpose. I remember asking deep questions at seven and eight years of age. Why am I here? What is my purpose? It was as if my soul was restless for me to grow up and do what I came here to do. When I look back on my life, every set back, every chance meeting was another step in the direction of finding my soul's purpose. When I am on purpose my soul is content and nourishes.

Why not go into silence and ask your soul what its purpose is? That silent inner knowing will never leave you alone until you open the door and listen to it.

"Purpose is something that was tucked away in your heart when you were born. Let it unfold."

CYNIC

Life's purpose meaning is defined by what you contributed to life. What will you be remembered for after you are dead? What did we learn from your life experiences? The cynic's life purpose means achieving something concrete, something to be remembered by.

I attended two very sad funerals of friends who had died prematurely in their fifties in the past year. I was struck by the difference in the remembrances people had of their interactions with the two men. For one, everyone spoke of his or her strong connection to this person. They spoke of his energy, his vitality, and his infectious love of life. His purpose seemed to be tied to his ability to reach out, to connect and to bring joy. He was much loved and sadly missed by a large number of people. I never saw so many adults crying openly as I did at his funeral.

In contrast, the people at the other funeral remembered a quiet, withdrawn, silent person. He was someone who had lived in a quiet, reserved, tight group. He was not one to reach out freely to people beyond his inner circle. He passed on quietly with few ripples on the pond. I found it hard to define his life's purpose or if he had achieved it. Oddly, I felt sadder at his passing as I felt he had not known his life's purpose and had passed through with little impact.

"Find your life's purpose and leave a legacy behind
you. Don't glide through life leaving no ripple."

2. Does everyone's soul have a purpose?

Soul

Every human being has a sacred quest to unfold his or her purpose. We are all here for a reason; there are no accidents. Don't let your ego get in the way and go out there striving and pushing. Why not let the true brilliance that is within you shine through you. If you are struggling to find your purpose, look back to when you were a child. What did you dream about? What did you like to do? It's funny how sometimes our life has to go full circle. Our deepest fear is not that we are inadequate, our deepest fear is that we are powerful beyond measure says Marianne Williamson in *A Return to Love*. It is our light, not our darkness that most frightens us. We ask ourselves, "Who am I to be brilliant, gorgeous, talented, fabulous? Actually, who are you not to be!"

Each one of you has the potential to truly change the world. Our souls are loaded with treasures waiting to awaken. Sometimes we can't see our soul's purpose because we carry too much baggage and search on the outside when our purpose lives on the inside.

I encourage you to let your soul shine through and your purpose will unfold. Acknowledge your greatness and recognise your divine gifts.

> *"When we live on purpose all matter of
> synchromystical experiences happen."*

CYNIC

To know your soul has a purpose, you first have to realise that you have a soul. Soulful people take the existence of a soul for granted. Big presumption! I too admire Marianne Williamson's words but wonder whether they refer to the soul or to the mind – the conscious mind.

I always have this conflict between wondering if it's my soul or my mind guiding me. Molly firmly believes that her soul is on constant duty working away on her behalf. I sometimes wonder if it isn't her overactive mind disguised as her soul. Whichever it is I have found that my life has more direction and meaning when I am living it on purpose rather than by a series of accidental happenings.

I reckon you would need to engage your mind fully before you could take Marianne Williamson's advice and begin to shine brightly. I have referred to that great poem in speeches to groups of women and it has always struck me that the women would be magnificent if they made a conscious decision to stand in their own power. What was missing was the conscious act of taking control and thinking about their purpose, then working to clarify the necessary steps to achieve it.

"Find your life's purpose and live it consciously or
you will live a life driven by short term goals"

3. HOW DO YOU FIND YOUR PURPOSE?

SOUL

Allow yourself time each day to meditate, dream, desire and imagine what your purpose is. Take time to look over your life. What was it you really enjoyed doing as a child? You can find enormous clues as to your soul's purpose by looking back at your childhood. When I look back at my childhood I realise I had started asking questions and reading about the soul from a very early age. I was fascinated by the deeper meaning of life. I also loved standing under a large oak tree in the Curraghmore Estate and pretending that I had a large audience of people to whom I was speaking. Make more statements every day about what you want in life and have the courage to let go of what you don't want anymore. Sometimes we have to make space in our lives for our purpose to find us.

Sometimes we can find our purpose from feedback from other people. I will never forget 2001 when I attended a large convention in Dallas. I met a man called Byrd Baggett, who tapped me on the shoulder and said, "Lady, you have the gift to touch people's souls." Four and a half years later I am now known as the Soul Woman.

"Let go and live in the moment."

CYNIC

In order to find your purpose you must take a good long look at your life and how you are living it. You need to ask yourself if you are happy and, most importantly, if you are healthy. I find that people who are constantly unhappy and/or unwell have a deep hole inside them, a lack of purpose in their lives.

Recognising my life's purpose has been an ongoing quest for me. I have always wanted to leave a mark as a result of my life. I always wanted to find my purpose in serving others in some way and always sought opportunities to do that. That can be a fraught life as you can end up living your life through others and end up drifting to other's agendas. I have realised in recent years that finding my own life's purpose is my own private task. It is also a top priority as it underlies so much else.

This has been brought home to me very strongly this year as I have watched many friends reach their fiftieth birthday and look around them and say, "Is this it?" They have realised that they are not living a life of purpose and been shocked into drastic actions like leaving marriages, leaving life long jobs, changing countries. They have gone on a journey in search of their life's purpose. They have had a crisis but they are confronting it. I have also seen friends who resist this hard task and continue to live a particular type of life, even though it is making them overweight or sick or tired, or in some cases all three. They will not examine their life to see if it is in tune with their inner purpose. It is heartbreaking to see someone you like moving from one illness to another as their body tries to tell them all is not well.

I often recommend that they read the book *Anatomy of the Spirit* by Caroline Myss, which points to the strong interconnection of mind to the well being of the body.

"Look and see if you can divine your purpose
in this life and if you are living it."

4. DOES EVERYONE HAVE A DESTINY?

SOUL

Yes, I passionately believe that when we are born our work is placed in our heart. It's something deep, deep inside. It's like a flame that illuminates and grows as you grow up in the world. Very often today, people sometimes feel that they are not on their destiny and ask me the question at seminars. I say to them: "Right now in your life, are you focussing on what you want to unfold in your life or what you don't want?" The reply is that they are focussing on scarcity and what they don't really want, which is what continues to show up in their lives. I heard a beautiful quote at Dr Jean Houston's Mystery School recently: "It takes a deep commitment to change, it takes an even greater commitment to grow." Fredella.

Have the courage to let go of what no longer works in your life and follow your destiny. It takes deep commitment and trust. However, you will live a much richer life as you weave your own tapestry. Bring your light to wherever you show up and your destiny will unfold.

Go out into your life and do what you came here to do.

"We are all born with a divine song inside of us."

CYNIC

Now there's a question! What is destiny? Is it a place where you arrive at the end of your life? Is that your destiny? Do you look back and say, "Yes, I have achieved my destiny", or do you take a more proactive view and say I will make my destiny.

I believe we do have a destiny but I like a more proactive view of it. Maybe it's because I've just turned fifty but I like to think I am making my own path. I think we learn from our mistakes, we mature, we grow and develop and we make new route maps. We are moving always towards our destiny but we have conscious control of our minds and our actions.

I would not like to think that I came on earth with a fingerprint on my forehead, which said this is your destiny, now go forth and achieve it. I disagree with Molly on this. I want more control. I want to choose my own destiny.

"Don't waste time wondering what you were destined for. Choose a great destiny and go make it."

5. WHAT IS DIFFERENCE BETWEEN DESTINY AND FATE?

SOUL

I see destiny as a path we walk down and make choices along the way. I see fate as something that has to and will happen; for example, we are all going to die and leave our bodies some day. Just as we are born into this world, we will leave this world. In this 21st century we have become obsessed with the body and ageing, from face lifts to tummy tucks. Yet no amount of plastic surgery can stop us ageing. It is fate that we all grow old.

My destiny is to touch people's souls and all the decisions I have made along the way have influenced that and taken me to where I am today. Fate is entirely different. I once heard a story about a man who felt he was fated to die on his 35th birthday, so he stayed at home all day, refused to go out or answer the door to anyone. In the evening, he was watching television when a bookshelf behind him fell on him and killed him. He could not escape death even though he felt he would be secure in his own home.

I love Robert Frost's poem *The Road Not Taken*. It explains choice and destiny to me.

> "Two roads diverged in a wood, and I-
> I took the one less travelled by,
> And that has made all the difference."

> *"Take the path less travelled."*

CYNIC

What a choice: destiny or fate. Having already said that I want to choose my destiny and my route map to it, what do I do about my fate? Fate for me can have a predetermined quality. You hear sayings like 'accept your fate' or 'it's your fate'. In Ireland, when someone dies young you often hear it said that it was his or her fate.

However, I have experienced the totally negative effect of a fatalistic approach on people's lives. In many desperately poor countries in the world, whole groups of people accept their fate as being preordained and they feel themselves powerless to do anything about it. They accept a life sentence of powerlessness and abject poverty because it is their fate. I feel myself getting angry about this and say, "It's not your fate. You can do something about it." However, when powerful interests exploit this fatalistic attitude they can control people's lives, from perpetuating an unjust caste system to sending young men and women to their deaths as suicide bombers.

So I feel whatever the evidence for my having a fate in life I prefer to keep a cynical attitude and say I'll make my own fate thank you very much.

"Don't take the easy, fatalistic route through life, you were born with a mind, use it to make your own fate."

6. HOW DO YOU KNOW YOU ARE ON PURPOSE?

SOUL

When we are soul conscious we are on purpose, we feel interconnected with the universe. We realise we are all one and we vibrate at a higher level. Teachers show up in your life to help you on your way. All matters of synchronicity unfold. You feel at peace with yourself and people around you and take responsibility for who and what you are. You are inspired and have an inner sense of knowing that all is well. You ignore what others think your purpose should be because you have a deep sense of knowing from inside that you are on purpose. You don't let your ego take over, you are in harmony with your thoughts. Your thoughts are clear and focussed and you know you are on the right path.

"It's time to show up in a big way in the world."

CYNIC

You know you are on purpose when everything connects and you feel a sense of coherence between the different aspects of your life. You know when you speak with someone who is not on purpose as you get a sense of them being all over the place. Nothing in their life connects. In fact, they can seem to be at odds with themselves.

I know when I am being pulled in a variety of directions in my business. I have said yes too many times and have not focussed. I find myself doing too many disparate things and being pulled off my purpose – the purpose of my business.

Knowing when you are on purpose in your life is harder to distinguish. Sadly, many of us do not know that our life may have a purpose and many die without ever having recognised it. If you are lucky enough to have looked for a purpose and even more fortunate to have found it then you will know.

I have found that this discovery of purpose often comes after sadness in your life and this newly discovered sense of purpose is therefore very precious.

"If you feel lost and wondering what on earth to do with your life, spend time deciding on your life's purpose".

7. HOW BIG CAN YOUR PURPOSE BE?

SOUL

Your purpose can be as big as you want it to be. I often hear people saying, "What am I supposed to be doing? I don't know if I have a purpose in life." Everyone has a purpose; it is no accident that you are living on this planet right now. I encourage you to stop worrying about how big your purpose is and just learn to let go and trust. It's something I have been doing in my life. For a period I thought I could control my purpose and see into the future. However, my purpose has found me in ways I would never have thought of and that purpose is actually bigger than I ever thought. Allow yourself each morning to hand over your day. Why not ask how you can be of service today and be mindful of what unfolds within your day. When you are of service to others it will nourish your soul and you will feel on purpose. There are no limits to what you can do here on this planet, only the limits you put on yourself. Let your purpose, like music deep inside of you, flow and find its own rhythm.

"Learn to trust in the mystery of life."

CYNIC

Your purpose can be as big as you need it to be. When you begin questioning yourself about why you are here on earth and what your purpose is, you might aim low and see a small purpose for yourself. I recommend you to see infinite possibilities, to aim for the stars, to realise the unimaginable. After all, it's your life, your purpose. So go deep, high and wide. Grasp the impossible and make your life's purpose become reality.

When deciding on your purpose it is useful to think of the following three pointers. Will I enjoy it? Will I be good at it? And finally, is it a little frightening? Eleanor Roosevelt said we should try to do something a little bit frightening every day. I think we should all choose a big enjoyable purpose that we can be good at and one which will thrill and frighten us. It is only when we are outside our comfort zones that we grow and achieve things which surprise us.

"Choose a purpose for your life which is enjoyable, and a little frightening."

8. Do Begrudgers Have a Role?

Soul

Begrudgers like to think they have a role but really they are toxic people. If you get into the habit of leading a toxic life your ego will continue to dominate your life. The soul is pure and is distinguishable from the begrudgers in heart by their thoughts and behaviour. Also remember begrudgers have a soul. Don't judge, just distance yourself lovingly from these people. We become who we hang out with all day long.

Many years ago I made a conscious decision to vibrate at a higher level and not hang out with people who criticised and moaned all day. Don't be pulled into their ways; just bless them and move on. When you send out negativity, that is what you will get back. When you send out love all illusions will disappear. I love a quote Dr Wayne Dwyer uses in his book *The Power of Intention*: "I attract only peace and peaceful people into my life." I agree with him. When that is what you focus on it works, that is what will show up in your life. The person whom you see as the begrudger in your life, what lesson have they come to teach you?

"Everyone you have a relationship with is a mirror of you."

CYNIC

They have a role whether we like it or not.

I imagine them to be like saboteurs waiting in the long grass for me. But you know they can be turned into a gift just by shifting your perception.

I imagine they are not sniping away, pouring negative energy all over me but 'reality checkers' sent to help me. Imagine that they are an unexpected gift. They will keep you grounded. They make you realise how lucky you are. Recently, I attended a wedding where the mother of the groom sniped away all day about the bride, who was considered not good enough for her precious son. It threatened to ruin the wedding. However, the sheer joy and love of the couple for each other completely overcame the begrudger. Their perception of the woman was that she was difficult but not a threat to their happiness or joy. They not only overcame her begrudgery, they obliterated it.

"Nil illegitimati te carborundum" or "Don't
let the bastards get you down."

9. IF YOU DON'T TAKE RESPONSIBILITY FOR YOUR LIFE, WHAT HAPPENS?

SOUL

Other people will spend their lives telling you what to do, you will be like a ship on a stormy sea, rocked to and fro, never feeling fulfilled. You might find yourself being dominated, unappreciated or taken for granted. What we put out in our lives we get back. The only way to go forward in life is to take responsibility for who and what you are. Everything that has happened in your life has happened for a reason, it has made you what you are today. Call your power back and feel yourself becoming stronger. Every morning and night, say the words, "No matter how much I protest I am totally responsible for everything that has happened in my life."

To move to the next level in your life you have to accept responsibility for what you are. You have learned the lessons, now go forward a lighter and more illuminated person.

"Stop saying 'someday', why not make that someday today?"

CYNIC

Every action you take is preceded by a thought. So if you think you are not responsible for yourself then you will behave as if nothing is your fault. You will think everything happens to you, you do not make things happen. You will develop the 'poor me' mentality.

You could drift through your whole life, year by year, until suddenly you are old and you wonder, *Where did the time go?* I turned fifty last year and it was a wonderful milestone. I thought to myself, *Well done, half a century and quite a lot done. But what next?* I like to tell myself that life is not a dress rehearsal. This is it. You get one chance at life. So seize it. Don't drift, don't shirk responsibility for yourself, don't waste your talents.

"Life is not a dress rehearsal. Take charge of yours now."

10. IS A QUESTIONING APPROACH GOOD?

SOUL

Yes, yes, yes! It encourages us as humans to delve deeper into the depths of why we are here.

> Who am I?
> Why am I here?
> What is my life's purpose?
> What brings me peace?

These are just some of the inspiring and thought-provoking questions you could ask yourself. Since my children have been little, I have welcomed their questions. Very often I don't have the answers. However, I do encourage them to go within and ask. My daughter Siobhan is nine, yet so confident in a solid sort of way. She is like a large candle flame flowing and shining brightly. My son, Declan, has a different approach to asking questions. He has a gentler approach and very often asks questions when I least expect. His candle flame burns in a gentle, deep and quiet way. Questions encourage us to scale and search who and why we are here.

"Sometimes when we stop to ask the deeper questions, they can take us home."

CYNIC

Great question.

I feel that sometimes in our lives we don't ask enough questions. Yet questions can take us to a magical place, also despair. What matters is how we perceive things. So many people sleep through their lives, always wanting the next big holiday or the next big thing, never stopping to enjoy the journey. A lot of people go to the grave with their music still inside of them. If only they had stopped to question themselves and find their purpose, maybe the music that is inside would begin to flow. Everyone's music is special and unique to the individual. That's what makes us all different and one large orchestra.

Look at children, how much they question everything with wonder. Unfortunately, too often they put it away by 7-8 years of age because we as parents haven't nurtured and encouraged this great gift. I never stop questioning. Often the questions I ask in the middle of the night are when my greatest answers unfold.

"You can never ask enough questions. It's only when you have a lot of answers that you can choose the best one."

11. HOW DO YOU KNOW YOU ARE ON YOUR PATH? HOW DO YOU GET IN TOUCH WITH YOUR SOUL'S PATH?

SOUL

The path we have to walk is not always easy. However, it's as if all manner of things come to help us; people show up to help us, the telephone rings, we get an invite and meet the person who helps us on our way again. At times we feel a real sense of inner peace, inner contentment. Those moments of peace and awe help us to get through the dark times. Learn to live each day with a sense of curious wonder and trust in the mystery called life.

I have learned in my life that being on the path is not about what I do in my life. It's all about learning just to be, instead of running around doing all the time. There is a message inside of you to learn to let go and the message will come out. Also, before I finish on this question, one last golden nugget I would like to share with you: let go of predicting your path, just learn to go with the flow.

There are various ways in which we can get in touch with our soul. One of the most relevant ways in my life has been through meditation. Each morning at 5.30 – 6.00am I wake and go down to our conservatory (which is a holy place for me) and I sit in the stillness of the early morning and prepare for the day ahead. I surrender to the universal presence, my day. Very often, when I am troubled, I will ask a question then wait. Sometimes the question won't be answered that morning. However, it always unfolds before the day is over. Magic unfolds every day in our lives but we are too busy rushing around to see it. Learn to be still; learn to get in touch with the holiness within you. Your soul lives in the stillness, it is waiting for you to speak to it.

Sometimes your soul will speak to you through other people. It happened to me in Dallas in 2001. I was at a large convention and didn't have the title for my second book. I had meditated and asked questions but still there was nothing. On the third day of the convention, however, I listened to a lady speaker from Texas who spoke about the blue flame. My heart jumped. I suddenly realised what was happening in the moment. My soul was getting a message to me through this lady on stage. My second book was to be called *The Little Blue Flame*.

"When you find your life's work it will not feel like another road but like a river – you will be flowing downstream pulled by the current."   Arrint

"A spiritual path has a flow to it, there is no place for the ego to live."

54

CYNIC

Everyone travels a path in life, whether consciously or unconsciously. For many of us it's an unconscious path, made up of routine and humdrum. We can get into the trap of working to eat, to go on holidays and then go back to work to eat and save for the next holiday. This is a hard path to be on. Yet many people live like this.

If this is you, now is the time to take your courage in your hands and ask yourself if you are surviving or thriving. If you think you are merely surviving then you are not yet on your 'path'. You need to rethink. Being on your path should have a sense of rightness and excitement about it. It should feel like you are living fully, thriving.

You can get in touch with your life's path when you begin to figure out what living a thriving life would look like. Would it mean working harder? Hardly. It more likely means spending more time with family and friends. I often wonder at people who spend their children's entire childhood on the road and then can't understand why their teenagers have no relationship with them. Their path of parenthood passed them by and they discover this too late. You only get a loan of your children for a short number of years.

Their path as a parent was crystal clear but they chose not to walk it. Many of my colleagues feel they missed out on that path. So your soul's path is often in front of you, it is the obvious path.

"Why survive when you could thrive?"

12. Does anyone ever die without figuring out their soul's path?

Soul

Some people sleep through the whole of their lives and never figure out their soul's path. Other people don't feel the need to question so deeply the reason they are here. My husband has never felt the need to search, study and explore the way I have all my life, yet he is completely at home with himself. The big question, "What happens after the soul dies?" is something most humans ask themselves at some stage in their lives. The greatest dread of death is the nothingness and the fear that death will end all associations with family and friends. I believe the soul lives on after our bodies die, the resonance of our energy lives on.

Since I was a child, I have sometimes been able to feel and hear messages from friends and families who have passed over. Recently, I spent the day with a friend who wanted some guidance as to her soul's purpose. She felt stuck and was searching for deeper meaning to her life. Whilst we were enjoying our coffee, I asked her about her friend's son, who had been killed in a car accident a year ago, and she told me that she wasn't coping very well. At that point our doorbell rang and when I went out there was no one there. I intuitively knew it was the boy's spirit at the door making contact so I invited him in and asked some questions. The answers were that he was okay but was worried about his mum and that he needed to move on. My friend said, "What will we do?" At that point the doorbell rang again and again. There was no one there. It was the spirit's way of letting us know that he wanted my friend to call his mum and let her know he was okay and well. His spirit had lived on after death, it's just that he didn't have a body anymore.

"When our work is done we go home."

CYNIC

Yes, frequently people die without even asking if their soul has a path. Many people live lives of quiet desperation. Yet they don't have to do this. We are ultimately responsible for ourselves, our thoughts and our actions. You can change at any point in your life. It's sad when you meet older people who say their life is all but over. They are in God's waiting room. I say it's not over until it's over so there is always time to do something different, to find your path.

I admire older people who sell all their life's possessions, accumulated over many years, and move to a new place to start a new life in a new climate. They feel they want to carve out a new path for themselves. Many have worked very hard all their lives and now want to do something else, like paint or travel.

"You should seek constantly until you find your path."

13. DO WE HAVE INTUITION? CAN WE TRUST OUR INTUITION?

SOUL

We are all born with intuition and a lot of people associate 'being intuitive' with 'being psychic' but it's very different. Intuition to me is about being very clear. Sometimes it comes as a voice. Have you ever heard that small voice inside you say, "Don't get involved with this person, be careful." Other times intuition comes as a vision. We have a dream or a déjà vu experience, and last but not least, you can experience intuition as vibration. When my husband and I were looking for a new house in 1993 we viewed our current house. Upon entering the property with the estate agent I could feel anger and raised voices. I later found out that the house had been repossessed and that the owner was so angry that he made sure he wrecked the house before they left. The neighbours then told me after we had moved in that they often heard shouting and arguments late at night. When the contracts were signed, the first thing I did was to go and cleanse the vibration of the house by smudging and Tibetan bells. We then created space for our energy, love and light to live in the house.

"Let go and live the life you were born to live."

When we have the courage to let go and trust our intuition our life flows. However, lots of people don't trust their intuition and get weary from going down cul-de-sacs because they refuse to face up to what they should be doing. Intuition is your friend and can help you flush out your life. When we trust our intuition it can bring messages from our soul.

One really useful affirmation is, "I will know whatever I need to know whenever I need to know it." There is a big difference between a belief and a knowing. Beliefs are something that you can be talked into or talked out of. A knowing is something that is part of you; it needs no validation and is part of your personal truth. When you trust your intuition then you will be given the information you need in your life in the proper time and way, allowing you to follow your soul's purpose. Why not work with what is happening now in your life and learn to interpret it instead of always chasing tomorrow's rainbow.

"Follow your intuition, believe in yourself – no one knows you better than you."

CYNIC

Everyone has intuition, but not to the same extent. There is a scale of intuition, ranging from little intuition through average intuition to high intuition. Very intuitive people can seem like they have second sight. They have the ability to see the big picture, to connect disparate facts into a comprehensible picture and to be futuristic. They make leaps of understanding and often don't know how they got to their new perception. It's like a gift.

Carl Jung's theories were further developed by Myers Briggs and they talk about the opposite of an intuition person being a sensory person. They are the ones with little intuition. They can often find the intuitive leaps maddening. Unlike intuitives they like to see a logical, connected link between one step and another. They frequently like to physically experience a situation before they really understand it.

Can we trust our intuition?

I completely trust this type of intuition, sometimes called your gut feeling.

I have seen it work many times when I have facilitated people to do strategic planning. You could pick out the high intuition people in the group as they would quickly grasp the future aspects of the plan and see the overview. Their contribution was vital. However, one has to be careful, as a drawback of people with this ability is that they can sometimes jump too quickly to conclusions, citing their gut feel as sufficient reason for their view.

"If you are having difficulty understanding a complex problem ask an intuitive person for help."

14. WHAT IS HAPPINESS?

SOUL

Happiness is a state of mind. However, many people today think happiness is a reaction to an event but actually it has very little to do with what is going on around us. Many people think happiness is in the next big house, car or something materialistic. However, when they do get whatever they are seeking they often find it empty. Happiness is an inside job: your soul is coded with happiness, it is our natural state. Everyone is capable of finding happiness, all he or she has to do is look for it in the right places.

Some people think happiness is overrated because they create guilt about being happy. Just recently I spoke at a large conference. I approached a lady who was looking very glum and asked her if she was looking forward to the conference. She replied, "No, because I have heard you speak before and you make people sing and dance." She was determined to plant seeds of doubt in my mind and not do the exercise where I encourage delegates to dance. Her parting words to me before the conference started were, "Nobody will dance you know, they are all going to walk out." So I stood up to do my keynote speech and decided not to start with the dancing exercise; I put the exercise at the end. I introduced the exercise saying, "If you can work together, you can dance together." Most of the audience laughed and let go and danced with their eyes closed. We are all God's children, we are meant to enjoy the wonders all around us. Happy people are the least self-absorbed and self-centred people among us. They volunteer their time to help others, are forgiving and often more caring than their unhappy counterparts.

"Happiness is all down to your thought processes."

CYNIC

Every day at every moment, we make the decision to be happy or not. I totally agree with Molly that it starts in our heads. For a number of years I worked visiting development projects in very poor countries in Africa and Asia where you would expect to find terrible unhappiness. Yet despite the appalling financial circumstances, I often found great dignity and a sense of contentment. I found this particularly in Africa where people were often happy for small things. They lived each moment, each day. I learnt a lot from these experiences. Happiness is not about possessions. It's much more to do with your state of mind, your contentment with your life, your place in the world.

It is such an ephemeral thing that it eludes many. It is so sad to see people of wealth and fame complaining about not being happy. So often, they just need to stop, to readjust their perceptions and their thinking. Don't you just want to tell the celebrities you see moaning on TV to get a life?

"If you decide to be happy then you will be happy."

5 Steps On How To Get In Touch With Your Life's Purpose

Soul

1. Look back on your early life.
   What were your dreams?
   What did you like to do?

2. Make a list of what no longer works in your life and let it go.

3. Take responsibility for who and what you are.

4. Take time out and ask yourself the deeper
   questions in life, for example,
   "Who am I?" and "What brings me peace?"

5. Trust your intuition.

Cynic

1. Don't waste time wondering what you are destined for.
   Actively choose a great destiny and go make it.

2. When choosing the purpose for your life choose one
   which is enjoyable, and a little frightening.

3. While making up your mind ask lots of questions. It's only when
   you have a lot of answers that you can choose the best one.

4. Think from a long term perspective or you will
   live a life driven by short term goals.

5. Check if you are surviving or thriving. You
   will be thriving if you are on purpose.

ARE YOU A CYNIC OR A SOUL?

THE QUESTIONS	CYNIC	SOUL
1. What does life purpose mean to cynic/soul?		
2. Does everyone's soul have a purpose?		
3. How do you find your purpose?		
4. Does everyone have a destiny?		
5. What is the difference between destiny and fate?		
6. How do you know you are on purpose?		
7. How big can your purpose be?		
8. Do begrudgers have a role?		
9. If you don't take responsibility for your life, what happens?		
10. Is a questioning approach good?		
11. How do you know you are on your path? How do you get in touch with your soul's path?		
12. Does anyone ever die without figuring out their soul's path?		
13. Do we have intuition? Can we trust intuition?		
14. What is happiness?		
SUBTOTAL		

CHAPTER 3: GET OUT OF YOUR OWN WAY... THE PRESENT

THE QUESTIONS

1. Why do people get stuck in the past?   66
2. Why do we sometimes stay
   stuck in what has ceased to work?   68
3. Do you regularly need to
   forget to look and leap anyway?   70
4. Are you in your own way?   72
5. How do you stay in your own way?   74
6. How important is your own
   estimation of yourself to your success?   76
7. Why do you let others sabotage you?   78
8. Why don't you get off your rear end and do it?   80
9. Why do you cod yourself?   82
10. Do you think setting goals is important?   84
11. How much does fear play a part in your life?   86
12. What do you fear most, success or failure?   88

5 STEPS ON HOW TO
   GET OUT OF YOUR OWN WAY   90

ARE YOU A CYNIC OR A SOUL?   91

1. WHY DO PEOPLE GET STUCK IN THE PAST?

SOUL

Fear is the number one factor that causes people to get stuck; it consumes them like a swarm of locusts. When we get stuck in the past we get caught up in what is history. We can never change the past: it is over. However, we can change the present moment. People who stay in the past use negative language like, "I can't", or "There have been too many mistakes" or

"That could never work because it did not work before". Listen to your inner speech, is it positive or negative? When you raise your energy level it again stops you from being stuck in the past.

I recently met a lady whose husband had died 20 years previous. At first I thought he was still alive because she spoke about Bill in the present tense. Her life had stopped flowing the day her husband had died. She still had all his clothes and belongings in the bedroom, pressed and dry cleaned since the day his soul had moved on. She was not only stuck in the past but still living there.

"Feel the fear and step into your life."

CYNIC

People get stuck in the past because they are terrified of the present, not to mention the future. Surprisingly, all kinds of people become stuck. Some seemingly successful people could be twice as successful, but are held back by having one foot in the past and one foot in the present. It always amazes me that people cannot let go of their experiences of the past. They seem to provide nourishment and comfort.

Many wounded people stay cowering in the past. The wound is too deep for them to move beyond it so they stay there nursing it. It is very sad to watch and to feel powerless to do anything. They need to decide themselves to let it go and to move on. I have a friend whose husband left her many years ago and she still gives a lot of her energy to that man and that period in her life. It is difficult for her to let it go.

I heard a wonderful speaker, Joe Calloway, at the 2004 National Speakers Association Annual Convention in Phoenix, who made an impassioned speech about 'letting it go'.

It was a rally call for all of us to move from our past. It was one of the most talked about speeches of the convention. Let it go has become a watchword for Molly and me.

Find the reason you can't move from the past. Expose it to the light of day and it will begin to lose its power over you.

> *"You can't have one foot on the shore and one foot on the boat… let one go."*

2. WHY DO WE SOMETIMES STAY STUCK IN WHAT HAS CEASED TO WORK?

SOUL

Very often the reason we stay stuck in what has ceased to work is fear holds us captive. Fear can keep us from living in the now and moving to the future. Our comfort zone also plays a big part in this. I experienced this struggle recently when I had to make some big decisions in my life. I had grown a successful, profitable training and consultancy business over 12 years, then in 2003 business began to slow down. I ignored the signs and my life's calling was also changing. However, I clung to the old ways for a period of time thinking I could dance in both worlds. That is, show up as the Soul Woman, my true calling, to select audiences, and also be the hard nosed business woman to the business world. Then one morning in January 2005 as I spoke to my business development manager, who was finding it very hard to generate new business, I realised my energy and passion had long ago left the consultancy side of my business. I made a decision to go forward that day and show up every day as the Soul Woman in business, at home, with friends, wherever I went. The result was amazing. Obstacles fell away and the phone started ringing with new opportunities for business. I had at last got out of my own way and surrendered to the magic of life.

"The past is an okay place to visit but sometimes a rotten place to live."

CYNIC

Change is one of the most frightening words in the English language. I find this so often that I often speak to people in business about transformation or transition rather than change as they seem to cope better with that approach.

It's simply easier to stay put in a relationship, a job or a city than to move. Moving means change. I think we should adopt an Alcoholics Anonymous approach and say, "I am Mary or whoever and I am afraid of change."

Clearly, if you know you need to change then you must have come through some process where you analysed your situation. Something may have happened that changed your perception and you said you'd had enough. Sadly, we do not ask enough questions, we do not look under the surface enough. We simply accept and put up with things.

Molly rarely stays stuck – she moves on fast! This is one of her least soul like qualities.

Cynics question and learn and so have the tools to move on from things that do not work but they can be lazy and having discovered the problem they start moaning about it instead of moving on. Soul people can often make a firm decision to soulfully put up with the problem: "It would hurt too many people if I changed so I'll be a martyr instead." Unfortunately, they often don't become quiet martyrs.

"Change means new opportunities."

3. DO YOU REGULARLY NEED TO FORGET TO LOOK AND LEAP ANYWAY?

SOUL

Yes, I believe you do, otherwise how would we ever learn and grow. As human beings we are designed to move forward, not stand still. I use my intuition, it's a small voice that lives within us all. Very often in life, we have to go to the edge and jump, not hold onto a twig. But we do. We continue to fool ourselves, we create illusions. How will you ever grow and stretch if you stay in the middle of your comfort zone, never taking chances? I encourage you to make a decision and take a leap in your life today, express your reality, it might be to change your thinking.

William James suggested:

> "Genius means making a shift in your thinking so that you let go of those habits and open yourself to possibilities of greatness."

So why not today take a leap and let your greatness out.

"Why not take one step forward right now?"

CYNIC

Well, now I'm not sure about leaping anyway. It depends on how well you looked beforehand.

I believe we should not jump blindly into things. We should examine all the angles first. I have seen people set up businesses on blind faith and go bust. From my twenty years in the not- for-profit sector. I have seen many people in voluntary agencies launch campaigns to help vulnerable people – with tragic consequences. They leapt and others suffered. Individuals can set up charities very easily and leap into fundraising, all because they want to help. They needed to do something. They don't think about realities like logistics, personnel or appropriateness of the aid.

I am not for people staying stuck and failing to take chances but the opposite is almost as bad. Jumping into a business or a relationship without thought is a bad idea.

The poet W.H. Auden in his poem *Leap Before You Look* put it well:

> The sense of danger must not disappear
> The way is certainly both short and steep
> However gradual it looks from here
> Look if you like, but you will have to leap

"Don't stay stuck but make sure you leap with your eyes open."

4. ARE YOU IN YOUR OWN WAY?

SOUL

Easy answer. I passionately believe that very often we get in our own way. We self-sabotage our own success. So many of us today keep pushing and striving and very often we then realise too late by asking what it has all been for. We get caught up in this spider's web that we spin around us, strangling us from going forward. So many people carry so much crap around with them that they become blinkered. For example, I'm not worthy; I'm not lovable; I'm not okay; I could never do that.

What lies deep inside of you is beautiful, not horrible. Learn to tell your ego to feck off and get out of your own way!

I want you to remember your value, know your worthiness and to love your life. You don't need to keep working so hard by staying in your own way. Let go and get in touch with your inner being. It is aware of your hopes and dreams and knows you better than anyone else.

"When we get out of our own way magic happens."

CYNIC

I agree with Molly on this one. We are all capable of standing full square in our own way. I once gave a keynote speech to a conference of Irishwomen working in agriculture entitled 'You would be great if you got out of your own way'. I talked about women having Venus flytraps in their lives. Flytraps they put in their path included fear of success, fear of failure, self-sabotage, and allowing negative people to constantly drain them.

I was overwhelmed by the positive feedback that I received. It really touched a cord with the women. Many freely admitted to me that they had not realised until then that they were completely blocking themselves. They simply had not stood in their own power. They thought they were being actively blocked from outside, but in fact they were the blocks themselves. The biggest block they had was not standing up and being counted. An economist working on generating information about Irish agriculture had written that there were more statistics about animals and land than about women in agriculture in Ireland. It was clear that these women needed to stand up and when they do they will be formidable.

"Find out how you are blocking yourself and stop it."

5. HOW DO YOU STAY IN YOUR OWN WAY?

SOUL

We stay in our own way by refusing to surrender to the next step in our lives. We as humans get so caught up in power, control and trying to make things happen, when actually the soul knows that most of our life can be lived with ease if only we would let go. Life will always unfold as it is supposed to. Very often I meet people who get in their own way and they are exhausted and unhappy from trying to win all the time.

I learned many times in my life that we can often make things worse if we don't get out of our own way. One story was how I knew from my soul that I would be part of the setting up of an institute in Northern England, so my ego took over and tried to make things happen. Nothing worked and I became more frustrated. Then one day, in September 2004, I surrendered during meditation. I handed over the unfolding of the institute and got out of my own way, mentally and physically exhausted. The following week I received a phonecall from a doctor whom I had met two years previously. He told me that he had just bought premises in the next village and that he supported my vision for the set up of the institute. When I let go of the illusion that control was good the universe had worked in a mystical way to take care of things.

"Stop living the life you don't belong in."

CYNIC

You stay in your own way by not facing up to reality. You can go through life without asking yourself any hard questions. You can just float along or worse, struggle along and never undergo any self-discovery or self-examination. We stay in our own way when we never question ourselves, never explore beneath the surface of our lives. You can say I don't have the tools to do that but that is a cop out. The tools are all around you and the first tool is the easiest: Ask questions. Never assume anything. In my courses, I always remind people that 'ASSUME makes an 'ASS' out of 'U' and 'ME'.

I had wanted to write and publish a book for a long time but had not done so. I moaned on and on and wished and wished until a friend of mine finally lost patience with me. He challenged me by asking me what was stopping me. You know the answer. Nothing, but myself: so he said to me, "Just do it – get out of your own way and do it." I was startled by this but did get out of my own way and my first book was published the following year.

Molly always tells people to get on with it and just do it. She is a wonder of determination. Look at her; if anything lands in her way she zaps it!

"Always face up to reality and then begin to deal with it."

6. HOW IMPORTANT IS YOUR OWN ESTIMATION OF YOURSELF TO YOUR SUCCESS?

SOUL

When you have high self esteem others will notice that and treat you in that way. As a soul I feel it is vital for success because when you respect yourself you won't be swayed by other's opinions. I encourage you to look in the mirror each day and say, "I like myself. I am confident. I am successful." If at first it feels strange, keep doing it." Sometimes in life we have to act before we become.

When I look back over my life I realise that a lot of my success today has happened because I believed I could, I believed I was a worthwhile person at first. However, I had to overcome years of limiting beliefs and conditioning. Everything that my life is today is because I held onto the dreams I had as a child and turned them into reality by sheer hard work and self belief. Why not buy some plain 3 x 5 cards today and write up ten positive traits that you have. Look at these cards every morning and evening. Carry them around with you until your subconscious mind believes anything is possible for you. If you first believe, you can.

"Stop pulling the rug from underneath yourself."

CYNIC

One of the earliest things I remember from my dad was his constant refrain to 'be confident as other people take you at your own estimation'. I love Eleanor Roosevelt's quote, which combines powerfully with my dad's: "No one can make you feel inferior without your consent."

My dad never read a self-help book in his life. He was born in 1910 and died in 1997. He was a very wise man and he gave me that gold nugget of wisdom for life. Unfortunately, it's easy to accept that point intellectually but a life's work to make it integral to your life. I now realise that probably one of the most important things that a parent can do for a child is to give them confidence and make them think a lot of themselves.

I see mothers all around me donating their life's blood to their children and yet still missing this vital ingredient. They drive them all over the city to classes, tutorials, football matches, all day and all weekend. Their children must learn music, dancing, sports, and drama. These things must be accomplished! However, the core element of self-confidence can be missed. The core feeling they have about themselves can be trampled in the rush to gain accomplishments.

No time is given to sitting with the child, going at the child's pace, building up their confidence. I know one woman who spends more of her afternoons and evenings on the road in her car, ferrying them around, than she does at home with them. What message does that send her children? If only they achieve all these skills they will be good enough – not a good message.

"People take you at your estimation."

7. WHY DO YOU LET OTHERS SABOTAGE YOU?

SOUL

We let others sabotage us when we give away our power to them. You let them drain your energy away. Sabotage happens because we associate power with social status, desire for approval, money. You then feel intimidated and threatened, which can lead to bad health. Your soul will never sabotage when you turn within and find the hidden genius within you, your life will be nourished again.

Stop letting yourself become over involved in other people's problems. When you learn to use your energy in a positive way, others will not be able to sabotage you. When you stand in your own power you won't have to try and please others, you will be grounded in your personal truth. Take a courageous leap of faith and walk through the sabotage of others. People are very good at letting us know why we should not do something. However, our true soul friends are the people who encourage us to move forward in our lives and hold our dreams with us.

It is only when you are discriminated from your soul that others will sabotage you. Take back the reins of your life and call your power back from this day forward.

"Take back the reins of your life and call your power back."

CYNIC

We let others sabotage us because we are not aware. It amazes me how we all let others sabotage us. We care too much about what others think of us and too little what we think of ourselves. We give power to other people when we do this – we give away our energy and our power too freely.

Have you ever thought about how you feel when you have been with a really negative person? Don't you feel drained?

We should remove these people's influence from our lives, blank them out. They are sabotaging us at our core. They are extinguishing our inner light and energy. Why then if we know how we feel after being with these people do we still let them zap us?

This is a question that I ask myself all the time. When I have an idea for a topic that I want to write or speak about I have learnt to guard it carefully. I only share it with a chosen few (positive) people.

"First identify, then remove all saboteurs from your life."

8. WHY DON'T YOU GET OFF YOUR REAR END AND DO IT?

SOUL

Laziness. Some people get into the habit of procrastinating and taking life easy. As human beings we are designed to move forward, not stand still. Action speaks louder than words. I encourage you to take the first step and move forward to the life that is waiting for you. Life begins at the end of our comfort zone. I encourage you to push your comfort zone out. You'll discover the change you want to see in your life. The first step is the hardest. Once you have walked the first few steps you'll begin to feel and act differently. Stop the excuses, as you can get off your backside and do it. Visualise yourself as to how it will be when you have achieved whatever it is you need to do. Take control of your moods and stop other people dictating or shaping your circumstances. Make a decision today and you can shape your life. When we get off our rear end, life ceases to be a rollercoaster and becomes more of a cruise.

"When you are feeling down, do something for
somebody else without telling anyone."

CYNIC

Starting is the most difficult aspect of any endeavour. Think how often you have procrastinated over going to your boss to ask for something; how often do you put off phoning a friend to come on holidays with you? We all suffer from this in some way. We are afraid of the change that this action will precipitate. So we do nothing. As long as we don't start it, it won't trouble us. A good idea is to do these tasks first in the day and get them over with.

Sometimes it's a matter of energy. You are just too tired to start something else. The spirit is willing but the body is weak. When this happens, it's always a signal to check if you are doing too much and might need to begin to prioritise. So I have learnt to be extra vigilant with myself when I know I need to start something difficult. Usually it is either good for me or necessary but I don't really like it so then I have to push myself really hard. Losing weight or taking up exercise must be the classic example of this. I would be slimmer, more energetic and feel better. So why don't I start going to the gym?

On a positive note I notice that I don't suffer from this inertia when I am involved in something I really enjoy. I get up and do all the initiating tasks willingly.

"Always do the things you like the least first. Then
you have the nice things to look forward to"

9. WHY DO YOU COD YOURSELF?

SOUL

Very often we cod ourselves because we are too afraid our light will shine too brightly – so we dim it. We are afraid of how magnificent we truly are. We spend our lives being busy, being average. Wake up! Nobody was born to be average.

Stop codding yourself and ignoring your deepest desires, getting caught up in useless gossip, overeating, overindulging and ignoring your inner voice. In my teenage years I yearned to belong. I codded myself into wanting to seek approval. That was until I realised I was disowning a large part of myself, my inner flame. Then my soul came knocking on the door and kept knocking until I opened up my gifts again. Why not make peace with yourself today? You will no longer have to pretend that you are someone you are not. Take down the barriers that you might have constructed around your inner flame and let your light shine brightly. The world needs your light in this 21st century.

"Step forth today from the dim light and let your light shine brightly."

CYNIC

I cod myself all the time. How else would I stay sane?

This question is particularly relevant to me because in the enneagram my type is asked this question as part of self-discovery. You are asked to give serious consideration to asking yourself, "How do I deceive myself?"

I feel we cod ourselves all the time about almost everything. Think for one moment about your day. When you look in the mirror in the morning are you pleased with what you see? Are you the right weight? Do you say I will do something about this or do you say, "Aah, it's only a bit of fat (all four stone of it)." Who is codding you now?

Then you go out to work and you say that you don't mind commuting for one to two hours as you love your job. "I don't mind leaving in the dark and returning in the dark." Ambitious people will often sacrifice their life to a career. Who is deceiving whom? Is your life not as important as your job?

Why do people stay in toxic relationships? Well, sometimes they cod themselves that things are not so bad or that things will get better. They can't face the reality, the break up, the loneliness, the failure, the loss of face. So they cod themselves.

Rollo May, psychologist, said: "The definition of insanity is doing the same things in the same way and hoping for something different."

"Don't commit the ultimate betrayal of continuing to cod yourself."

10. DO YOU THINK SETTING GOALS IS IMPORTANT?

SOUL

I prefer to use the expression 'setting intention' instead of goals. Many years ago I was very goal orientated and pushed and strived to make those goals happen, often to the detriment of those around me. Intention is different. When you set intention, it's not something you do but rather getting in touch with the universe, the invisible field of energy that exists all around us. When you set an intention you live as if it is already here and believe it will come to pass, you don't need to focus on the 'how'; leave that up to the universe.

In 2002 during morning meditation, the words 'United Nations' passed through my mind and somehow, from that moment, I knew I would one day be called to speak at the United Nations. I put the words United Nations up on my story board in my office. In March 2005, I attended the Mystery School in New York, run by Dr Jean Houston and on the second morning of the programme I was having breakfast with a group of women and sharing with them some ideas about my work. When I had finished a lady across the table took out a business card and said that she worked for the United Nations and that she would like to speak to me. The outcome is that I have been asked to speak at the United Nations in New York in 2006. When we learn to live in alignment with our souls and sue the power of intention we begin to live mythically.

"Learn to trust in the mystery of life."

CYNIC

Setting goals is vital. I have learnt this the hard way. It is very easy just to coast along, being busy and the years pass by.

The only way to achieve the important things in your life is to sit down and think of what you want to achieve. Think in the future for you. Make your future in your future. Fast forward five to ten years and ask yourself, "Where will I be in ten years? What will I be doing? How will I look?" Then work back through the years to the present.

This is the essence of goal setting and if you don't do this you will drift. When you set your goals it impacts on every decision you make today. You begin to ask yourself, "Will this help me reach my goal or not?" For example, if you decide you want to have a thriving business, say, you want to be the owner of a chain of shops in ten years time, then every decision, every day will bring you either closer to that objective or not. Your ten-year goal starts to impact on today. So if someone asks you to travel around the world with them for a year, you have to decide whether this will bring you closer or farther from achieving your goal of owning a business or not. You may say no, not now.

If someone asks you to work with them in a health spa and you dream of opening a chain of shops selling beauty products, now that's a different decision. You may say, yes, that will help me along the path to my goal.

"If you are failing to plan you are planning to fail"

11. HOW MUCH DOES FEAR PLAY A PART IN YOUR LIFE?

SOUL

Fear does not exist in the soul. Fear lives only in the ego. The soul overcomes fear by stepping into it. Fear cannot attach itself to the soul because the soul vibrates at a higher level. The soul knows that you are powerful beyond measure. Fear cannot exist where love flows, love cuts the cord of fear. The soul acknowledges your greatness when you own up to what you are. Then you will walk in the presence of God.

The Soul is that part of you that is your true self; it wears no masks so it has no fears.

"Learn to look at F.E.A.R. as Feeling Excited And Ready."

CYNIC

If you are brutally honest with yourself you will find fear lurks in the most unexpected places. I feel fear plays a bigger part than we realise in our lives. Fear of change is one of the big fears I encounter in my work. You must be honest with yourself, strip away the outer layers and ask yourself, "Why am I doing what I am doing? Am I content? Am I surviving or thriving?" If you answer, "I am not thriving", then go deeper and see if fear is holding you back. Often it is. Fear of changing your cosy set up can hold you back. I know this place, I am familiar with this job, I am comfortable with these people. If all the statements contain elements of comfort, ease, familiarity, then you are no longer challenging yourself. If so, you must ask if fear of change is at the heart of this.

It is only when you are feeling a sense of challenge, a sense of discomfort, of your abilities being stretched and tested that you are learning. In facing challenges you grow. I encourage you to realise the fear is there but to harness it and use it.

It helps greatly when you imagine that you are on a continuum. At one end, pulling you forward, is your desire to do something different. At the other end is the feeling of unhappiness at your situation. Imagine you are in the middle. Which is motivating you more, the desire to go forward to a happier place or the desire to run away from unhappiness? You can be motivated in either of these two ways: desire to move on or fear staying until staying is worse than going. One is a thrust forward while the other is a move from a negative situation.

"Never let fear take over your life."

12. WHAT DO YOU FEAR MOST, SUCCESS OR FAILURE?

SOUL

The soul doesn't experience or feel fear because it doesn't live there. The soul vibrates at a higher level where only light, collaboration and success exist. The soul also never makes comparisons. When we make comparisons it is the shortest route to unhappiness. There is no problem or situation that the soul cannot deal with. As humans we are a mass of contradictions. We get to choose in life so it's up to each and every one of us whether we choose success or failure. Life is a school where we encounter successes and failures along the way and when we have encountered them all, we return home to that state of soul where comparisons don't matter or exist. We realise it was all only a great illusion.

"Fear and failure is all a great illusion that you create inside your head."

CYNIC

Most of us learn early in our lives that we fear failure. We realise early that we don't like to look foolish in front of others. We fear being different, being judged. Children will often opt out of sport or drama if they feel they may draw attention to themselves.

So we are all familiar with failure from an early age. What we need to explore is the numbing effect this fear may be having on our initiative, or on our creativity. I have come to realise that fear of failure is a waste of time and effort. I firmly believe that I only learn when I test myself. I seek out opportunities to work in different countries and with different people because I know I will learn. I may well be frightened of the size of the challenge but I know I will learn from the failure as well as the success. I recently discovered that in Bosnia Herzegovina they speak of this as needing to have a stone in your shoe.

In recent years, I discovered the evil twin sister of fear of failure. It's called fear of success. I had not realised that this could be a fear holding me back. In my childhood we were encouraged not to boast or 'show off'. We celebrated success lightly and moved on. This discouraged us from seeing success as something to shout about. In effect, we were taught not to shine too brightly.

When I read Marianne Williamson's words in her piece *Our Deepest Fear*, I realised that fear of shining too brightly was clear. This fear fosters and supports self-sabotage.

"Our deepest fear is not that we are inadequate. Our deepest fear is that we are powerful beyond measure. It is our light, not our darkness that most frightens us."

You take on something new, you are getting good at it, and you are beginning to succeed. You have exceeded your wildest dreams and suddenly you do something that is an act of pure self sabotage. Don't do this to yourself.

"Examine your past year and see if you can spot the twin
– fear of failure and fear of success in your life"

5 Steps On How To Get Out Of Your Own Way

SOUL

1. Let go of the past, it's a great place to visit but a rotten place to live.

2. If you wear the victim tee shirt, take it off and burn it.

3. Stay away from people who pull you down in life.

4. Stop living the life you don't belong in.

5. Why not call your power back today?

CYNIC

1. Look on change as a new beginning, a wonderful opportunity.

2. Don't be afraid to leap into something but do keep your eyes open.

3. First identify the main internal things which are blocking you, then work to eliminate them.

4. Always think well of yourself as people take you at your own estimation.

5. Examine your past year and see if you can spot the twins – fear of failure and fear of success in your life.

ARE YOU A CYNIC OR A SOUL?

THE QUESTIONS	CYNIC	SOUL
1. Why do people get stuck in the past?		
2. Why do we sometimes stay stuck in what has ceased to work?		
3. Do you regularly need to forget to look and leap anyway?		
4. Are you in your own way?		
5. How do you stay in your own way?		
6. How important is your own estimation of yourself to your success?		
7. Why do you let others sabotage you?		
8. Why don't you get off your rear end and do it?		
9. Why do you cod yourself?		
10. Do you think setting goals is important?		
11. How much does fear play a part in your life?		
12. What do you fear most, success or failure?		
SUBTOTAL		

CHAPTER 4: REVIEW AND RENEW YOUR RELATIONSHIPS

THE QUESTIONS

1. Can our independence survive our relationships?   94
2. Why don't we just move on?   96
3. Can the past influence your future relationships?   98
4. Should you know yourself first –
   then your relationships?   100
5. Can relationships be transformational?   102
6. What are the ingredients of a good relationship?   104
7. What stops people from letting go?   106
8. Do nitpickers get a bad press?   108
9. What do we do with the angry types?   110
10. Is your soul destined to be with certain people?   112
11. Is your soul destined to have certain children?   114
12. Does love conquer all?   116
13. What do you do with the precious people?   118
14. Can you be happy living alone?   120

5 STEPS ON HOW TO REVIEW
    AND RENEW YOUR RELATIONSHIPS   122

ARE YOU A CYNIC OR A SOUL?   123

1. CAN OUR INDEPENDENCE SURVIVE OUR RELATIONSHIPS?

SOUL

From the soul's point of view we need to be independent, to learn and to grow and to love. When we are attached it is the root of fear, and fear and love cannot co-exist. In today's society we are fed with the idea that in order to be happy we should form relationships of attachment. When we are independent in our relationships we overcome worry, anxiety and tension, which drains the energy of our consciousness and over time could poison our relationships.

When we are aware of ourselves as spiritual beings we are attached yet unattached and independent to everything that shows up in our lives. When we rediscover our real authentic self our relationship with others blossoms.

Detach yourself from the need to hold on to things and people. My husband and two children are my rock in this world yet I do not own them. My inner knowledge tells me they are on their own paths just as I am on mine and being married to my husband for fifteen years is part of the journey. We are both very different people yet we complement each other. He allows me to grow as I need to and I allow him to do the things that he needs to in life. To me this is unconditional love, which doesn't demand that anyone of us is right or wrong, we just are. It is our independence that has helped our relationship to grow and flourish.

"We are spiritual beings having a human experience."

CYNIC

True independence can survive anything and should not be threatened by a relationship. I find people can confuse independence with self-centredness. They think 'I can do what I like because I am an independent person'. Not so. That is a limited view of things; independence is a wonderful thing if it means being self-reliant, doing your own thing and coming thoughtfully to your own conclusions.

If you are an independent thinker, your own person and not dependent on other people to mind you, then you are a lucky person. Many people spend half their lives coming to this place.

So if you then enter a relationship can you maintain your independence of thought and action? Well for many people this is a crunch point. All good relationships are based on compromise and cooperation so to become a unit of two parts some sort of trade off naturally occurs. If your independence is a mature, grown up, well-balanced approach to life you will find a way to preserve it while co-existing with another. If your independence is of the self-centred and immature type, you will find co-existing more difficult. You may see a relationship with all the strings attached as a threat to you.

"It is possible to retain true independence but not self-centredness while having a fulfilling relationship."

2. WHY DON'T WE JUST MOVE ON?

SOUL

Very often we don't move on because it becomes a great excuse in our lives not to move forward. We become victims and somehow get power from the attention we get from being stuck in the past. Holding on can be a great cover for fear. When we don't let go we are often afraid of the next step, it could be success, sex or intimacy. Whenever we recognise what it is that frightens us we begin to let go.

If you are finding it hard right now to move on from something in your life, why not appraise the problem. What is holding you back? Recognise your style of holding on. Whatever your style is, imagine putting this in the higher state of your mind – hand it over. By doing so, you let go of the now, in order to move forward.

"The past is over, live in the present and you make your tomorrow."

CYNIC

I feel very sad for people who get stuck after a relationship has broken down. They can become victims of the breakdown, staying in one place, unable to move on. We have seen this in Ireland when people are killed in violent ways and twenty years on their relations are still in the same place. It is a very sad thing to behold.

Then there are others who forgive and move on. They don't forget but they truly forgive and find a way to move onto a new and different life. Why don't we just move on from sadness, upset and trauma? Well, sometimes we are too wounded. We have lost some big part of ourselves. I know when my sister died unexpectedly within months of my father and brother dying I was not able to move on. I was too overcome with grief, too shocked by the sudden and unexpected death. It took me a number of years to really get over it and move on. But luckily I did.

I wonder if not moving on may sometimes be due to people wanting to use the wound and paradoxically drawing strength and meaning from it. It begins to define them so it is hard to let go.

"Life is a journey – a serious of moves. Try not to get stuck midway along in your journey."

3. CAN THE PAST INFLUENCE YOUR FUTURE RELATIONSHIPS?

SOUL

When we don't learn the lessons from our past relationships it can influence our future relationships. The lessons we do not learn in our early relationships with our parents and subsequent relationships show up again and again until we learn them. I have been working with people for over 22 years now and I see how patterns go on to repeat themselves.

One lady that attended my seminars was desperate to settle down and form a stable relationship. She had three previous broken marriages and had 'desperate' written on her forehead, which meant that when she went out to the local bars most men could read the signals and would not enter a long term relationship with her. Too quickly she became possessive and needy when she entered a new relationship and the same pattern would unfold all over again. I encouraged her to look at her past relationships and current relationship and look at what she was trying to take from each. She quickly realised that she had been trying to find in others what she had not found within herself – love and acceptance. When she spent time learning to love and accept herself she was then ready to love and accept others in any relationship she encountered. She had broken the relationship of a lifetime and was ready to walk into the future and create new rewarding relationships.

"Learn to stop trying to control or fix other people, instead focus on your light."

CYNIC

Yes, we never really escape our past. It is always inside us. So how could it not influence our future?

The key point with past relationships is whether they were good or bad and how we learnt from them. Take business relationships. I entered a business partnership a few years ago and then realised after a year it was not really working. It was not a real partnership: it was too unequal. So I ended it and moved on with my business. Did it influence my future relationships? Definitely. I was always wary of people who wanted to work in a partnership with me. I realised that partnership is a very loose term, open to many different interpretations. Many of them fell short of what I considered real partnerships. So I have found other ways of working with people but avoided the partnership route.

I particularly like the idea of not hanging on to past arguments or hurts. I like Oscar Wilde's words:

> "Always forgive your enemies,
> nothing annoys them so much."

"Learn from your past relationships, forgive any failures and move on."

4. SHOULD YOU KNOW YOURSELF FIRST – THEN YOUR RELATIONSHIPS?

SOUL

I began the search of knowing myself very early in my life and yes, I believe it has helped me in my relationships. When we meet someone who is comfortable in their own skin they ooze peace and serenity.

I remember attending a weekend in Southern Ireland when I was 15 years old. The course began on a Friday night and as you checked in you handed over your watch. It was a weekend of exploration and deep searching through stories, games, singing and lectures. I remember writing inside my notebook *I've got to be me to be free* and for many years afterwards I wrote it in all my journals, until a few years ago I wrote *I am me, I am free!*.

When you truly know yourself you can then liberate and allow everyone else you meet along the way top be themselves. You don't need to fix, change or dislike the unique traits in everyone else.

No one can ever truly know you as well as you know yourself. Similarly, you can never get within someone else's world. However, you can be there truly for someone else and listen to their world when you have come home to yourself.

"Knowing yourself will set you free."

CYNIC

You should definitely learn to know yourself first. I am amazed each day at people's lack of self-knowledge. How they are locked into patterns of behaviour stemming form childhood. I have seen female friends form relationships with the same type of male friend again and again with the same sad ending. The common denominator is the mindset of the woman. They do not know or understand themselves so therefore are very bad at picking people worthy of their friendship and love.

Knowing yourself is a life's journey and we are always making some new discovery. Big challenges can allow us to find strengths that we did not know we had. If we don't embark on that journey we will never learn all the facets to our personality. We need to know ourselves before we go out and interact with others. How can you begin to control your own behaviour if you don't know yourself? We don't want to remain prisoners of our predictable behaviour; we want to know and control our behaviour. Thus, when we know ourselves we have a better chance of building lasting relationships.

"Know yourself first then go out and interact with others."

5. CAN RELATIONSHIPS BE TRANSFORMATIONAL?

SOUL

When we take responsibility for our lives and our choices, relationships can be transformed. A few years ago I had a difference that I had never sorted with my uncle and he was dying. One evening, a few months before he died, I called the hospital and asked the nurses if they would bring the phone to his bedside and we talked in a very open way. I told him how much I loved him unconditionally and that I didn't bear any grudges about matters of the past. Our relationship was transformed that evening and a few months later when he was on his deathbed my mother called to say that she felt he was holding on to speak to me again. I asked my mother to put the phone up to his ear as he was in and out of consciousness and we went on a transformational journey together to the next world where he went home. By following the principle of transformational communication you can heal yourself of the past, that is trying to be healed in the present.

"Transformation will come when you let go of your attachments."

CYNIC

Every interaction with another human being can potentially transform us.

I like Carl Jung's words:

> "The meeting of two personalities is like the contact between two chemical substances: if there is any reaction both are transformed."

The real question is, "In what way will the interaction transform us?"

It all depends on how to open other's influence. If we are rigidly locked into a certain viewpoint and behaviour we can be like a Teflon coated pot; everything will run off us. I always love to meet new people; I see it as a way to learn something new everyday. It is good to look at each new relationship as a potential force for change in your life. Unexpected transformations can come from unusual relationships, like the challenge that comes from getting an older and wiser mentor. Someone who will give you constructive feedback.

"Have at least one relationship in your life where you get honest and constructive feedback."

6. WHAT ARE THE INGREDIENTS OF A GOOD RELATIONSHIP?

SOUL

Trust and openness are the key ingredients to a good relationship. Trust is consciously putting our energy behind something knowing it will work to our benefit no matter how it looks. When we trust, good things happen. Many people start out loving each other but after years of frustration and sometimes disappointment their passion dies. When we are open to our partner we open our hearts to greater forgiveness and an increased motivation to give and receive.

Relationships can also be magic. When we realise we are different and we give each other room to grow. I have been married for 15 years. My husband likes motor bikes, rugby and rock music. I like meditation, reading and flowers, yet we make space for each other. The feminine part of me needs to share everything with him and he over the years has listened to me. The male in him likes fast motor bikes and I give him space to enjoy his bike and his rugby. Relationships are all about give and take and have to be consistently worked at.

"When you are in the flow you inspire others and draw people to you."

CYNIC

Good relationships are made of two sides coming together in an equal and respectful way. The equality aspect is crucial to a sustainable relationship. Mutual respect and regard are vital as is a bond of trust. When the relationship deepens to an intimate one these elements must be present but will be strengthened by love.

I see many relationships, marriages, long-term partnerships, where the couple profess love to each other but there is no mutual respect or trust. So the love is undermined by this lack of respect or turns into manipulative or destructive behaviour.

This basic respect and trust must exist even in work and professional relationships. I find its absence can be at the bottom of bullying, exploitation and negative relationships in work. You should seriously question any relationship where there is no respect and trust. You must have standards and keep to them for your own survival.

*"Always look for respect and trust as fundamentals
in any relationship – business or personal"*

7. WHAT STOPS PEOPLE FROM LETTING GO?

SOUL

Neediness is very often what stops us from letting go. We become attached to someone or something because deep down inside we become afraid that we would not be complete without them.

We want to keep controlling, holding on to the pain, attachments and desires. Sometimes it can become so real for us that without it we fear there would be nothing or no one there. We fear non-existence. When relationships go wrong it can be very painful for one or both of the people concerned. When you can't let go of something it steals a huge amount of your energy. Your thoughts become fuzzy and it's as if the other person consumes you.

I encourage you to let go of any anger, greed, lust, money issues, power or ownership you have over another. Love is the most important force in the world. Call your power back now. When you let go and detach the neediness you will find that you will learn to love people more deeply in an unconditional way and you will experience deep inner peace rather than inner turmoil.

"Let go of control and forgive yourself."

CYNIC

People fail to let go because they are afraid. They need the security of the familiar even if it is painful. It is a great shame when people don't move on. A new phrase much in use now is 'build a bridge and get over it'. I think it's vital to find the bricks and start building.

One of my friends stayed in a work position for 15 years, slowly getting more and more destroyed. He moved from discouraged through dismayed to almost discarded. Still he stayed. I talked to him and realised he was terrified of change. He is still there and probably will be until his employer makes the decision for him.

"Letting go is the most liberating feeling."

8. DO NITPICKERS GET A BAD PRESS?

SOUL

Yes and no. Some people who ask a lot of deep questions get labelled as nitpickers when in fact they are really just trying to process information to understand the whole picture. However, some people nitpick in a destructive way to bring people down and ruin their reputation. They spread gossip and lies about them; very often they do this because of their own inadequacies or because they are jealous or envious of that person. When we nitpick in a destructive way, it brings a lower level of consciousness into our life like control, greed, lust, fear, envy and blame. Make a conscious effort to keep away from people who nitpick in a destructive way. Keep your energy up, vibrate at a higher level. Be conscious in your thoughts that when you nitpick it's contagious; make sure you are not spreading it.

"When people heal spontaneously they go to that special place inside."

CYNIC

Nitpickers are nature's way of keeping up standards. The free flowing visionary spirits need nitpickers coming along behind them making sure everything is in place to make the vision happen. Without the nitpicker we would have little compliance with standards. They proofread excellently, do accurate tots of figures first time round, always balance their bank statements and keep computers running.

They counterbalance the creative types with much needed detail and accuracy. I know the free flowing soul, guided by signs from the deep, does not welcome the cynic pointing out practicalities or raising obstacles. It's a low level frequency trying to tempt the free spirit to earth.

Whenever I write something I give it to my favourite nitpicker and I am confident that he will find all the flaws and inconsistencies. What a wonderful contribution from my husband.

*"Everyone needs to develop the ability check
details – excellence is in the details"*

9. WHAT DO WE DO WITH THE ANGRY TYPES?

SOUL

The only answer I have to that question is to give out love and send love. Do not get caught up and consumed by someone else's anger. Anger wastes our energy, it brings doubt and fear into our life, it creates a resonance of tension.

Many years ago I was running a workshop in Edinburgh. A gentleman on the workshop made a very personal comment about women. In that moment all the other delegates, also men, looked at me in stunned silence to see what my reaction was going to be. I paused and thought to myself, I wonder what's happening for that person right now in their lives. I didn't react. I responded to the gentleman in a gentle voice and moved on with the workshop. During the coffee break the same gentleman approached me and told me that he was going through a divorce and wanted to lash out at someone. I listened with compassion to him and what a wonderful human being he was. When we encounter angry people, remember, it is their anger not yours. Learn to hear what they are saying, all the time sending love. The same gentleman wrote to my office a year later to say he had found a new companion and that life was good. Who knows where you will touch someone's life?

"When we are not in a loving state we bring forth the negative side of our behaviour."

CYNIC

Some people are completely comfortable with anger – it is second nature to them. Anger comes from their inner core. They are either angry with the world or angry with themselves. Perfectionists can be very angry people, only the anger is directed inside at their failure to meet their own impossibly high standards.

There are many public figures who you can count on to be angry, almost angry on demand. They end up in politics, trade unions, or fighting for the people of the Third World. When I worked in a Third World development agency I became very familiar with the 'eternally angry' types. They had a deep but mobile anger, which they transferred from Africa to Asia to Ireland, depending on the cause that caught their eye. This type of righteous anger can be very useful; it can move mountains but only if used carefully. Constant vocal anger can lose its potency with overuse.

I am happy to mobilise people's anger in a good cause but I am not happy when people overlook the negative effect of their anger on others.

"Anger used in a good cause is powerful but anger used personally can be devastating."

10. IS YOUR SOUL DESTINED TO BE WITH CERTAIN PEOPLE?

SOUL

When we have a connection with another soul at a deep level it's as if there is an awakening, a sense of ancient knowing, you come home to each other. Destiny unfolds and you become one. The one you love, your anam cára, reflects back to you, your own soul. We do have a choice and sometimes, people today make a choice to be friends instead of love partners. Some people's souls are more awakened than others.

About five years ago I met an old soul friend and could clearly see and understand our past life history. However, they were still in deep slumber and unaware of the connection. We cannot fill up our emptiness with possessions and people; we have to go deeper into that emptiness. Only love can fill that space.

Yes, I do believe that we are destined to be with certain people, to learn the intimate lessons we need so that we can become more fully human, fully alive.

"When you meet another anam cára, it's as if you come home to yourself."

CYNIC

I don't know if your soul id destined to be with certain people. It smacks a little of a predetermination which I find difficult to accept. I believe we make decisions at every moment of the day and each decision affects our life and our relationships. So I think we have too many choices to actually accept that there is a predetermined set of people we will end up with.

Sometimes people say you were determined to end up with your husband and you have been together for almost 30 years. But I say that's not a destiny, that's the result of a series of choices made every day.

I have friends who, in their fifties, separate from their partner of 25 years and I feel so sad for them. Was it his or her destiny to spend half a life with someone and then end up all alone? I don't know but it seems to be they must have made quite a few choices in those 25 years which led them to their current situation.

"Many people come into your life but you actively decide who will stay there."

11. IS YOUR SOUL DESTINED TO HAVE CERTAIN CHILDREN?

SOUL

I believe we belong to soul groups and each child chooses before they come into this life who their parents are and what lessons they want to learn. Just as a parent teaches a child, we also learn from our children.

I had a very strange experience when I was carrying my second child. Up until six months of the pregnancy I had a deep inner knowing that I was carrying a little boy and his name was Conor. Then one night, nearing the end of my sixth month, I felt a shift in my womb. It was if I wasn't carrying a boy anymore but the soul of a little girl. By now I had bought some new Peter Rabbit vests and baby grows. I went with some friends to see a medium and she said she saw my aura surrounded in pink and that I was carrying a little girl.

"Our children are the light bearers of tomorrow."

CYNIC

The idea that your soul is destined to have certain children opens up the nature/nurture debate. How much influence do I have over my children with my interactions with them and how much is due to hereditary factors? Undoubtedly, we have profound effects on our children. We are models for them from their earliest days. We teach them by our example. So that will profoundly influence a child growing up in a household where arguments, fighting and violence are the norm. They may even begin to see that as normal. On the contrary, a child brought up in loving, supportive family set up will have a different view of life.

So yes, we are destined to have a certain type of child. Genetics are undeniable. We have a huge influence by what we do and what we don't do over our children. It is vital that we do the best we can. I have heard it said that parents are given a child at birth on a loan until they reach adulthood when they are gone. So you need to make the most of every moment of the time your children are with you.

"You only have your children for a short time. Use it well."

12. DOES LOVE CONQUER ALL?

SOUL

Yes, love does conquer all. When love touches a human soul it changes it forever. The eyes, which are the windows of the soul, take on a brilliance that is not of this world, for pure love comes from a source which only we can feel.

We can draw from this never-ending energy; like attracts like.

Everyone and everything needs love.

Love can heal years of hurt and anger and set someone free.

Mother Theresa once said:

> "We cannot do great things in life. We can only do small things with great love."

Love is what gives order and sense to life. Love is what brings us together and brings us to God.

If you want to feel satisfied in life, that you have made a real contribution and to be remembered, then care for yourself and others. Love truly conquers all, it is the circle called life.

"Love is what gives order and sense to life."

CYNIC

I would like to think love conquers all but unfortunately my life experience tells me it doesn't. Love is a potent force, which can envelop you as Molly suggests. It can push things forward and change people. However, to believe love conquers all makes you reliant on this blind force. I prefer to think that a questioning approach to life leads to true understanding of other people.

I have seen conflict situations where no resolution would have been possible if you had gone in with pure love. You would have been thrown straight back out. What worked was questioning and listening, especially lots of listening.

Only when both sides really understood the other did they accept the other. Then, after acceptance, came forgiveness and finally regard. Rushing in with love would not have worked.

> *"Love, if backed up by an intelligent well thought*
> *strategy, may well conquer all."*

13. WHAT DO YOU DO WITH THE PRECIOUS PEOPLE?

SOUL

Precious people are sometimes governed by their moods. We all have a choice as to how we respond to these people, whatever they throw at us. I recently encountered a person who would be called precious whilst I was working in America. My initial reaction was to wonder what was happening to that person right now after they had verbally attacked me. Then I realised they were consumed by fear. At first, when I had encouraged them to let go, they barked at me and gave me a look as if I had gone mad. I continued to walk in their shoes and try and see the world from their point of view, not my own. Always, always make the other person your starting point. Have there been times in your life when you have been precious? It's only a label that we humans give to a mood or state of mind.

A week after returning from the States I received a letter from the person I had worked with thanking me for helping her have a major breakthrough. When we are willing to be truly there for another human being all matters of magic can happen. Next time you think someone is precious take a good look at yourself first.

"Perceptions can enrich or condemn other people."

CYNIC

Precious people for me are the ones for whom life is never enough. They are always searching for something. They find it hard to settle for what they have and be happy. They seek the really special object, the really special experience, the really special person.

When they go on holidays, they tell you of the remote island only they found, the special beach only they visited, the unique pieces of pottery only they found because the pottery closed after they left. You get the picture. What do you do with these people? Well clearly you can't change them. They seem to have a deep yearning inside them to find and experience things at a deeper level. It can be frustrating being with these people. You want a coffee but they will walk half an hour to find the place with the Kenyan double brewed coffee served in blue mugs. You have to accept them. But instead of getting mad try humour. Try to send them up to make them see how extreme they can become and how selfish this makes them appear.

"Some people live a life of deep yearning for meaning. Use humour at every opportunity to lighten the load."

14. CAN YOU BE HAPPY LIVING ALONE?

SOUL

Only in solitude can you truly find out who you are. In solitude you come upon your own beauty. When you inhabit your solitude fully you realise at the heart of it is neither loneliness nor emptiness. I had a few uncles who never married and were very happy living alone. In fact, one uncle believed life was much less complicated because he didn't have to worry about anyone else. Some people would see that as selfish. However, I honour his decision to live his own life. How often today do people crave to get away from all the hustle and bustle of life? In the Celtic world there has always been the recognition of silence and we believe in Ireland that an invisible presence walks the road of life with us. So are we ever truly alone?

*"The real key to life is to live in the mystery
and embrace our inner stillness."*

CYNIC

I know I would not survive all alone because I get my energy and zest for life from other people. I light up when I am meeting people and look forward to company. I was once asked to ponder this question to see if I was an extrovert or introvert in the sense of where I found my energy. If you were tired at the end of the day, which would you rather do, go home to a bath and bed or go out with friends and chat? You know the answer. The introverts go home to bed and bath and the extroverts go out.

I have several friends who have carved out full lives but who have chosen to live alone. They have done this for so long now that I doubt they could cope with the compromises needed to co-exist with others. I travel a good deal in my work and I look forward to going home and sharing all my experiences with my family. It is a huge part of my pleasure in the trips. I could not imagine not having anyone at home to share these things with.

"Being alone can be as much a state of mind as a physical reality."

5 Steps On How To Review And Renew Your Relationships

Soul

1. Stop trying to fix or control other people.

2. Take responsibility for all the choices you have made in your life so far.

3. Don't let others anger consume you – practice responding with love.

4. Get to love and understand yourself more every day that you live.

5. Trust and openness are the two ingredients to great relationships.

Cynic

1. Live fully by keeping your independence while simultaneously building a strong shared relationship.

2. Forgive transgressions, learn from them and move on.

3. Work hard to know and understand yourself – self discovery is vital..

4. Always try to stand in the other person's shoes and see things from their point of view.

5. Give and receive trust and respect in equal measure.

ARE YOU A CYNIC OR A SOUL?

THE QUESTIONS	CYNIC	SOUL
1. Can our independence survive our relationships?		
2. Why don't we just move on?		
3. Can the past influence your future relationships?		
4. Should you know yourself first then your relationships?		
5. Can relationships be transformational?		
6. What are the ingredients of a good relationship?		
7. What stops people from letting go?		
8. Do nitpickers get a bad press?		
9. What do we do with the angry types?		
10. Is your soul destined to be with certain people?		
11. Is your soul destined to have certain children?		
12. Does love conquer all?		
13. What do you do with the precious people?		
14. Can you be happy living alone?		
SUBTOTAL		

CHAPTER 5: WHAT LEGACY WILL WE LEAVE?

THE QUESTIONS

1. What do you want to be remembered for?   126
2. Does everyone leave a legacy?   128
3. What happens when the body dies?   130
4. How do you see time?   132
5. What is the number one truth you tell your children?   134
6. Should you live each day as if it were your last?   136
7. What is forgiveness?   138
8. Do we need to forgive before we die?   140
9. How do you view death?   142
10. Does work-life balance matter?   144

5 STEPS TO HELP YOU EXPLORE
  WHAT LEGACY YOU WILL LEAVE   146

ARE YOU A CYNIC OR A SOUL?   147

1. WHAT DO YOU WANT TO BE REMEMBERED FOR?

SOUL

Wow! What a deep question. OK, hold on a minute, let me get centred and still. As I write the answer to this question it is 6.36am. I am sitting in a caravan in the Findhorn Community tucked away in the north east of Scotland. OK, back to the question. I would like to be remembered as a flame of light that touched people's souls and encouraged them to shine even brighter in this world. We are all here for such a short time on this planet yet we very often think we are here forever. Why is it bad news happens to other people or other people die but not us? Let's get real and realise our time here is precious and what resonance do you want to leave behind? What would you like people to say about you? What habits would you like to see your children continue long after you are gone? How will you have touched people's lives?

"The world is dying to hear your voice – this is the century."

CYNIC

I was really struck by the question in Stephen Covey's book *The Seven Habits of Highly Effective People*, where he asked you to imagine standing at your own graveside and asking yourself, "What do I want to be remembered for?." I thought this a life-changing question.

Unfortunately, as you get older you find that you are attending more funerals and always this question arises in one form or another. "How do you remember the deceased and how did they touch your life?" It's a good discipline to fast forward to the end and to ask yourself that question. Then when you answer it, plan to achieve it. You must convince yourself that you have control over that.

I want to be remembered as someone who contributed to people's lives, who helped them reach the place they dreamed of being. I know when my sister died suddenly and totally unexpectedly we were devastated. But we knew she had left a wonderful legacy – her children and grandchildren, who were the centre of her life. Her legacy lives on everyday in them. I would like to feel that when my time comes. I would have changed lives and that will be my legacy.

"Think of what you want people to say at your graveside and work back to today."

2. Does everyone leave a legacy?

SOUL

We all leave a resonance in different ways, some through our children, poetry, music, laughter, stories that others go on to tell long after you have gone home. In Ireland, I was brought up with a wonderful tradition, the Irish Wake. When anyone dies in the family the funeral is a holy experience, where the body of the person is usually waked in their own home and people come to accompany the body through its first night of death. Some drink and lots of stories are shared about the person. I have even been to a wake where traditional music is played. We view death as a celebration, generally everyone in the village goes to the funeral and long after the funeral is over the person's legacy lives on in the village in one way or another. The Irish often keep the legacy of someone who has died by sharing stories around the fire on a cold winter's night, then the children go on to tell their children and the legacy lives on in the hearts and minds of the people.

*"Your legacy lives on in the hearts and minds of the
people you have encountered in your life."*

CYNIC

Do we leave a legacy? I'm not sure about this. It's more that certain individuals make such a big impact in life that when they go they leave a big hole and you look around in sorrow and see their touch everywhere. Their legacy is in things, places, people and changed attitudes. A good friend of mine, Glenda Wilson, died some years ago after a heroic fight against cancer. She was someone who had a profound effect on me with her open and generous spirit. At her funeral in New York and her memorial service in Ireland, her legacy was everywhere. You heard it in all the stories people told about her, about all the quiet kindnesses, unexpected gifts, thoughtful calls or letters. Her open love and affection for all her vast array of friends was everywhere. This was her living legacy.

Unfortunately, I have also seen the legacy of bad people who are mean spirited and spend their life hurting others. On a recent trip to Bosnia Herzegovina, the legacy of the atrocities committed by evil men in rape camps and ethnically cleansed villages is still palpable in the air and the faces of the people. Their legacy is inescapable and will blight generations to come.

Sometimes an evil legacy can damage people so much that they need a soul to come and help them heal. The cynic would probable say 'show me and I will believe' but after seeing some of these places I hope and trust in something greater than me coming to help heal these people.

I always find comfort in the words of Emily Dickinson's poem: *If I can stop one heart from breaking.*

> "If I can stop one heart from breaking,
> I shall not live in vain;
> If I can ease one life the aching,
> Or cool one pain,
> Or help one lonely person
> Into happiness again
> I shall not live in vain."

"If you can stop one heart from breaking, then
you have started to build your legacy."

3. WHAT HAPPENS WHEN THE BODY DIES?

SOUL

The robe that is our body falls away and our soul is free. The soul is that holy part of us that is imperishable and eternal. Death is only a physical phenomenon. When we die it is as if we move from one room to another; you won't need a body you will need a point of light. The resonance of who you were will live on. Since I was a young child I could walk between both worlds. There is a thin veil between the world of the dead and the world of the living. Just because we don't have a body does not mean we don't exist anymore. Over the years, I have had many visits from people who had been close to me but who had passed over. The most recent was when I attended Mystery School in Port Jersey, upstate New York. I fell into bed at 11.30pm, tired from travelling and I had the most vivid conversation with Fr Jimmy O'Connell, who had been one of my greatest mentors. In my sleep I could see him clearly and smell him. He guided me as to what my next step should be – setting up a soul school in England. When I awoke at 5.15 the next morning, I had information and insights that I had not had before. I also know from conversations with him that his body is now free from pain.

"Death is only a physical phenomenon."

CYNIC

The light goes out and life ends. The physical matter of our bodies returns to its natural elements. If you believe like I do that everything is energy, that even solids are vibrating with energy at the subatomic level then you have to see the answer in terms of energy.

When you die the energy of your body stops and you are left with the basic elements. They return to the energy chain and they are reabsorbed.

I was brought up in the fifties and sixties in Ireland in a strongly Catholic tradition and culture. I was firmly taught that we all have souls and that our souls live after our body dies. How you lived your life influenced the final destination of your soul.

I have never moved away from the idea of having a soul but I feel I now have a less theological view of it.

If you believe that there is some higher force directing and pulsating through life then when the body dies the life force must rejoin that greater force.

I know Molly, my soul friend, believes that souls visit us many times and we can see them again and again. In fact they often visit her when she is with me but they are wise enough not to appear to the cynic. Molly firmly believes in past lives. I have never asked her about mine, as I prefer not to know. I'm afraid that I might have been here before as an unsavoury character.

"Energy always reunites with energy."

4. How do you see time?

SOUL

Time is man-made. Time does not really exist. The past, present and the future is happening right now. Man gets caught up in time constraints and then stresses himself. It is very important how we use time. Too many people spend their lives stuck in the past or trying to live in the future. The best way to view time is to live in the now and do one thing at a time. You can get control of your time and your life only by changing the way you think, work and deal with the never-ending river of responsibilities that flow over you each day. One of my disciplines is to take 'me time' each day. It centres me and gives great depth to my life, which means I can be there for others.

"Time is a man-made thing."

CYNIC

I see time as something that I don't have enough of and I realise that is the wrong attitude. There is the same amount of time for all of us; the challenge is how we use it. All good time managers tell you to grab time by the scruff of the neck and make it work for you. Otherwise it drifts away.

When I was in my twenties I thought that I had a lifetime in front of me and so did not panic about achievements. I set myself the goal of seeing a great deal of the world by the time I was forty. Luckily the right career unfolded, which allowed me to reach that goal.

Now I see time as limited and frequently say that life is not a dress rehearsal so stop practising for your real life. Get on with it; you might not be here tomorrow.

Time is a very precious commodity in my life and so I feel I should use it well and achieve a good work life balance.

While Molly gets her me time in her meditation and her communing with souls the cynic is up and out walking the roads. I wonder if she has an edge with the me time?

"You have as much time as the next person – use it as wisely as you can."

5. WHAT IS THE NUMBER ONE TRUTH YOU TELL YOUR CHILDREN?

SOUL

Love one another – love conquers all. Love overcomes all arguments, fear and hatred. Love to me is a state of grace, there is a holiness to life, it creates a presence inside us of peace, warmth and non judgement.

Love encourages us to take risks, to grow, to reach, to search. It creates positive energy and we vibrate at a higher consciousness. Whatever you do in your life, do it with love. When you wash up, wash up with joy, when you drive your car, drive it with love. Love creates a healing energy where we are all one.

Human beings need another human being. We are all connected on a cellular level, let it be with love. When we receive love we celebrate love with gratitude.

Love other people the way you want to be loved. Give everything you have and you will be a rich person.

"Love other people the way you want to be loved."

CYNIC

I constantly tell my children that people take you at your own estimation, so think and know that you are the best you can be and people will take their cue from you. I tell my children to trust in themselves and their gifts.

I have told them to realise the full potential of life and to live it knowing what they are good at. I encourage them not to accept other's views of them as their starting point but to go inside themselves and find their own strengths.

I am not so sure about love conquering all as I have seen too many dysfunctional people ready to pull you down if you appear to shine too brightly. I tell my children to start with themselves and then to look at others but never to accept what they see on the surface. I encourage them always to go deeper and to seek the real person, the real explanation, and the real problem. To do this you must be centered in yourself and you must be self aware.

To live and work well with others you must first understand yourself and have self-esteem. You can't truly love others if you don't love yourself first.

With this in mind I have tried to bring them up to know that there are multiple intelligences as discovered by Howard Gardner. I want them to know that they are excellent in certain ways but that it is all right not to shine at everything. I want them to know about all eight intelligences as discussed in his great book *Multiple Intelligences*. I particularly want them to know about intrapersonal and interpersonal intelligences, as they will then understand the importance of knowing yourself and of being able to interact well with others.

I want them to understand the many dimensions to growing up and to being a successful adult. I think that I have tried to put being an 'emotionally intelligent' person as a top priority for my children.

Funny enough when I asked my 21-year-old daughter to answer this, she said without question that I had told her not to marry a rugby player or other match- playing sportsman who would put his sport before her.

"Do not accept other people's views of you. Instead
go inside and find your own strengths."

135

6. SHOULD YOU LIVE EACH DAY AS IF IT WERE YOUR LAST?

SOUL

The soul lives for today and knows that tomorrow will take care of itself. There is no need to rush. Why not just live one moment after another, enjoying each moment . Time is an illusion, the soul is eternal. Nothing exists outside the now, the now as you read these lines. My question to you is, "If you only had today, this day as you read this book, how would you live it?" When we live each day as if it is our last, we get less stressed about life. It's amazing how the trivia falls away from our lives. We don't get caught up in the shoulds and ought to's in our lives. We do more of what we want to create in our lives and less of what we don't want in our lives.

Fear finds it very hard to live in the now, the present moment. When you look back on your life, it is the moments and the days of magic that you will remember. I can still remember special moments as far back as six years of age such as going down to visit my granny on the back of my dad's large, black bike that had a little red seat on the back for me to jump up on to. And I would throw my arms around my daddy's waist and hold on tight as he cycled down the beautiful estate to my granny's house in the village. As soon as we got there she would always have a glass of milk and a slice of bread and butter with sugar on it.

Why not now take a moment and look back at some of the special days you have already lived in your life.

"We are the ones we have been waiting for — live it."

CYNIC

I always live every day as if it were my last. In all reality it could be.

I was struck ice cold by a poem by the American poet, W.S. Merwin, called *The Anniversary of My Death*, in which he raises the possibility that in the past year I have passed over the very day that will turn out to be the anniversary of my death. He says:

> "Every year without knowing it I have passed the day
> When the last fires will wave to me
> And the silence will set out
> Tireless traveller
> Like the beam of a lightless star"

He sees the end of life as the fires waving at him. If you think like this you move your perception of death from being an abstraction to it being a concrete reality. So having moved to that place it seems easy to then think of living every day as if it were your last.

When you come to this place in your mind it seems a good idea to try your best every day and to make it have a purpose, even if it is taking a day off to rebuild your energy. It also makes sense not to go to bed on your anger or with any row unresolved. I always believe in making peace before I go to sleep.

I know that the soul Molly will see life as a continuum and that she will be back again. I think being here once is hard enough so I go for the short term, rather than the 'rotating soul' approach.

"If you live every day as if it were your last you will have one fun life."

7. WHAT IS FORGIVENESS?

SOUL

To me, forgiveness is a letting go of pain and suffering. It's as if we take the invisible rucksack off our back, empty the contents out and make a choice that we no longer want to carry the anger, despair, hurt or grief that we might have been carrying.

Forgiveness is being able to view everything and everyone in a non-judgemental fashion. I love the quote in Marianne Williams's book *A Return To Love*:

> I forgive you.
> I release you to the Holy Spirit.

Another great affirmation that you could say every morning and evening is:

> Dear God,
>
> Please take my thoughts and feelings about xxxx. Use them
> for your purpose. Let this relationship unfold according to
> your will.

If you make it a discipline in your life to use the above affirmation in times of trouble, whatever it is you are finding it hard to forgive will disappear. Hand it over to God and see what unfolds.

"Tears of forgiveness allow us to feel connected and move forward
in a way that heals our life and the world around us."

CYNIC

Forgiveness is receiving the hurt, letting it pass through you and refusing to let it dwell in your life. Then looking to the person who hurt you and saying I will not hold this against you, I will let it go and in so doing release you from the hurt you have inflicted on me. I will forgive you. It will not be a life-defining issue for me. I can move beyond it.

For me, forgiveness is part of being a grown-up, fully developed adult. It is as much about you as it is about the person hurting you. I have always been very influenced by Nelson Mandela's total forgiveness of his oppressors. Right from the beginning of his long imprisonment he remained detached, he kept his soul intact, they never got him. His forgiveness gave him enormous power. I thought his autobiography one of the most influential books I have ever read. It was a manual in forgiveness.

I realise that forgiving a wrong is also one of the most difficult acts possible. I have seen people caught in the throes of blame and anger, as I myself have been. I have wasted time trying to understand why people would want to hurt me, but now I build a bridge and move on. I don't dwell on it.

"Learn from Nelson Mandela and forgive all your enemies."

8. DO WE NEED TO FORGIVE BEFORE WE DIE?

SOUL

Yes we do. However, for some people it is very hard to forgive. We become stuck in no man's land. Our hours and days pass in darkness, then sometimes that hate, anger and despair can turn to disease.

When we forgive it sets us free of attachments. Before you can ever hope to forgive another person you need to forgive yourself and when you let go of years of limitation it is as if you see God at work. You as a human soul will bloom again, just like the first daffodils of spring and with it comes a radiance and compassion so strong.

I had to learn forgiveness at a very early age. My uncle had abused my trust. I focussed on my uncle's good points and through the pain of forgiveness love shone through. He was in fact one of my greatest teachers. Sometimes the person we need to forgive can be great teachers. "What lessons do we need to learn?" That's a question I always ask myself during my darkest times.

"When we forgive it sets our soul free."

CYNIC

Not only do we need to forgive before we die, we need to forgive right now. Carrying around resentments and anger at someone else is corrosive to your inner self. It is not possible to move on if your whole life is bounded by the dark emotions inside you. However, some injustices can be so heinous that it can be almost impossible to surmount them. In Northern Ireland in my lifetime there have been truly awful atrocities, so awful you felt that the world had descended into hell. Yet always a forgiving person would emerge and show the way by shining forth.

One instance was when there was a terrible bombing in Enniskillen in 1987 where 11 people were killed. One man, Gordon Wilson, was standing with his daughter, Marie, and he was fine but she was killed. In the immediate aftermath, there was terrible anger, hurt, rage even, but then I heard him on radio saying he forgave them. It stopped a whole nation. The power of his simple words was astonishing.

He was an amazing man and he showed the way.

"Carrying around resentments is a waste of your energy, let them all go."

9. How do you view death?

SOUL

We are all going to die one day but who amongst us really believes it? We all know in our souls it's going to happen yet we pretend it's not. Our soul views death as an opportunity for growth. Death is like a sandcastle that is washed away with the changing tides of time. The soul views death as a transformation, a passage to the next world. I love the Tibetan tradition of death that says we must all live up to death. This means living up to the truth of death. It also means living each moment instead of sleepwalking through our lives.

Many years ago I was in a pub in the west of Ireland and an old man said to me, "What's the difference between all those people who are buried across the road in the graveyard and us?" After he slowly took another sip of Guinness, his reply was, "Time, that's the only thing, one day we will be there too."

"From the moment we are born we are dying, living our life's work then going home to where we came from."

CYNIC

In recent years a number of immediate family members and some close friends have died. The shock of losing so many key people in my life has made me stop and think about death in totally concrete and real terms. I now believe that until you really suffer grief at first hand you can continue to discuss death in abstract terms. Once you have felt its icy tentacles it becomes a grim factor in your life and influences your subsequent outlook on life.

Now I see death first and foremost as a huge loss. Someone you loved is gone, absolutely gone. It is the absoluteness of that departure that is hard to fathom. Your conscious mind does not accept it, cannot accept it. It still sees the person in shops, hears them in the garden, smells their perfume. So death is a loss, a gap, and a void. For a long time after my mother died I could not go into a large shopping centre in Dublin, as it was where I had met my mum every week to go shopping. It was unbearable as I kept seeing my mother at different places in the centre waiting for me as she always did. It was later that I discovered that my sister had exactly the same reluctance to go into the centre.

Gradually, you move on and begin to think of a longer time frame – of a God and a destiny. Slowly, one can see the longer view, the inescapability of death, the plan. Eventually, you come to the view that they may not be really gone just altered – in a new energy state. But don't rush yourself to this perception, it comes in its own time. There is nothing more wounding than pushing that longer term view onto a recently bereaved person, however well meaning the intention. I have a serious respect for the devastating effect of death on people and now walk very carefully around bereaved people, always taking my cue from them.

"Death is a huge loss and grief must be deeply respected."

10. DOES WORK-LIFE BALANCE MATTER?

SOUL

Life is full of ups and downs, good days and bad days, things that work out and things that don't. Work-life balance is essential for a happy and contented life. A state of well being exists when we have balance in our lives. If we lead an unbalanced life then stress, illness and unhappiness will be the result. Doing work that you don't like, treating yourself badly, eating unhealthily, being in a poor relationship, can all have a powerful influence over our health.

In 1997, I became caught up in hurry sickness. I was going, going, going. I thought I could be superwoman. I thrived on being a human doing and never stopped to recharge until one day my body could take no more and I got serious back pain. I hadn't listened to the symptoms from months earlier, the niggling pains in my lower back. So in January 1998 I tried to get out of bed and found my lower back had seized up. It took me six weeks of visiting a chiropractor to learn to be a human being again.

In the West today, many people have no idea what truly good health and wellbeing feels like. Despite our higher standards of living there are many influences that damage our work life balance; the long hours work culture, noise pollution, materialism, processed food, etc. We need to stop and get off the merry-go-round. To have fun, sleep well, exercise and nourish our soul.

"We all have 'to do' lists every day. Maybe it's time to create a 'stop doing' list."

CYNIC

Getting a good work-life balance is the most important aspect of any person's life. I know that finding a fair balance can be hard. It is all too easy to keep saying yes to work demands and to allow that to encroach on your life. I recently spoke at a conference of young accountants who were only just waking up to the idea that work-life balance might be an issue for them. They spoke glibly of working weeks of 80 to 100 hours, long commutes and increasing stress.

What really frightened me was the powerlessness of these 20 and 30-year-olds. Their acceptance of this way of life was absolute. They didn't realise that they were actually handing over their spiritual, mental and physical health to others. Most of them welcomed any quick fix solutions on how to reduce stress or to regain control temporarily but I really doubted that many of them actually realised the importance of work-life balance to their fundamental wellbeing.

To me. work life balance is the starting point in planning my life. I know that if I don't factor in my own leisure and my family's needs at the beginning then they will end up in second place. So Molly is right about the 'human doing' but I suspect she would have us all mediating in our balanced time whereas I might open a glass of merlot.

"Make achieving a work life balance the number one priority in your life."

5 Steps To Help You Explore
What Legacy You Will Leave

Soul

1. Ask yourself this question right now: "If this was to be your last day on earth, how would I live it?" Journal your answers.

2. Practise living in the moment each day – you will find that you have many more moments to enjoy, one after the other.

3. Take time today to look over your life. Is there anyone you still need to forgive? Why not call them or write to them now?

4. What areas of your life need more balance right now? Explore the following: work, family and friends, health and fitness, and 'me' time.

5. Before you read the next chapter, create a Stop Doing list now.

Cynic

1. Think of what you want people to say at your graveside and start living towards it now.

2. Don't complain about not having enough time. You have as much time as everyone else. You must learn to use it wisely.

3. Make having a work-life balance your number one priority. Do it now.

4. Stop carrying around hurts and resentments. They use up valuable energy. Let them go.

5. Live every day fully, as if it were your last.

Are You A Cynic Or A Soul?

THE QUESTIONS	CYNIC	SOUL
1. What do you want to be remembered for?		
2. Does everyone leave a legacy?		
3. What happens when the body dies?		
4. How do you see time?		
5. What is the number one truth you tell your children?		
6. Should you live each day as if it were your last?		
7. What is forgiveness?		
8. Do we need to forgive before we die?		
9. How do you view death?		
10. Does work-life balance matter?		
SUBTOTAL		

CHAPTER 6: CYNIC OR SOUL - SYMBIOSIS OR SABOTAGE

THE QUESTIONS

1. How do cynics/souls manage their energy? 150
2. How can the soul survive in the cynic's world? 152
3. Is the cynic the shadow of the soul? 154
4. Can one survive the other? 156
5. Can appearances be deceptive? 158
6. What are the three steps to being a cynic or a soul? 160
7. Can you take yourself too seriously? Can you overdo it? 162
8. What are the strengths of both? 164
9. Soul/Cynic index (continuum) 166
10. How can you be both a cynic and a soul? 168
11. Will the 21st century be the century of the cynic or the soul? 170

5 STEPS TO SYMBIOSIS OR SABOTAGE 172

ARE YOU A CYNIC OR A SOUL 173

1. HOW DO CYNICS/SOULS MANAGE THEIR ENERGY?

SOUL

The soul is energy and sees everything in life as energy. When you meet another person your soul exchanges energy with the soul of the other person. Your soul will manage your energy well. However, if you choose to view life from the cynic's point then you could be left feeling lethargic and drained. Why not learn to take time and go to the still, quiet place where the soul lives and ask the soul to replenish your energy. The soul's energy is love and only love. Anything else will drain you in life.

Meditation and regular discipline will help you to live by your soul and stop the cynics stealing your energy. The soul's energy is concentrated, mindful and purposeful, whereas the cynic's energy is very often jumbled and chaotic.

"Everything in life is energy."

CYNIC

Aha – a clear soul view! The cynic's energy can be deadly when focussed on a particular outcome. The cynic sees the energy source and uses it to a purpose. They don't just live, it they use it.

Enough with the love and only love. What about the people you can't stand? The cynic would walk away from the negative energy and apply himself or herself more productively elsewhere. Cynics are not burdened with the need to love everyone they can take or leave people and so be wise about the energy they donate to people.

"Use your energy wisely. It is one of your most precious assets."

2. HOW CAN THE SOUL SURVIVE IN THE CYNIC'S WORLD?

SOUL

The soul survives in a cynic's world by meditating and finding quiet time. Meditation nourishes the soul, as food nourishes our body. Meditation can also be done in various ways. I walk every morning for about one hour and my walking is a meditation, a quiet time in preparation for my day ahead. The soul also flows and becomes when you mediate on nature, a beautiful sunset or sunrise. Find what's right for you. You are a soul, you are eternal, your soul never dies. Your flame might get diminished when you get caught up with the hype or negativity of others but it is always there, like a pinpoint of radiant light. Soul consciousness is the key to taking charge of what goes on in your mind.

"What happens inside our world is what we will create outside."

CYNIC

The soul needs to go warily into the cynic's world. Many cynics would have trouble with all that quiet nourishment. I can appreciate the need to find and value quiet and stillness but would want to put some structure and order onto it. I would need to take charge of what goes on in my mind in a strategic, analytic and purposeful way.

The soul would need to lighten up a little and come some way from the mediation to the market place or risk ending up soul unconscious!

"Meditate and find peace, then spring into planning mode."

3. IS THE CYNIC THE SHADOW OF THE SOUL?

SOUL

I believe there is ying and yang to everything in life. A caterpillar will become a breathtakingly beautiful butterfly. Jung was the first person to give us the term 'shadow' to refer to those parts of our personality that have been rejected out of fear, ignorance, shame and lack of love. Very often I see the shadow as the person we would like not to be seen as. When I need to lose weight the soul part of me will easily see the slim me, the person whose belly doesn't hang out or down as you get older. The cynic in me tells me to get real, I am way overweight and these feelings sabotage my self esteem unless I grab hold of them. It's as if there is a war within my head – one side pulls me back while the other encourages me to go forward.

"We are all possibilities of consciousness."

CYNIC

No way! The cynic is not the shadow; that is too dark a view. The cynic is objective, questioning, balanced, lives in the overview and tries to keep the soul under control.

Where would we be if we trusted everything to the inner soul? We would be in a peaceful, still cul-de-sac. I understand the ying and yang and the war in our heads. However, the soul likes to be the dominant force and can see the cynic as a threat. In fact, it is not a threat. Anything but!

The answer to the war is to let the cynic have its place alongside the soul. The two seem to occur in everyone, although one seems to dominate. The challenge is to give them equal space.

"Recognise that you have a cynic and a soul. Give them both space."

4. CAN ONE SURVIVE THE OTHER?

SOUL

Willpower and discipline is needed. Both have a part to play in all of our lives and too much of either can be a bad thing. The cynic in all of us can wear many faces, controlling, critical, judgemental, selfish. The soul can also wear many faces: fluffy, easy going, non judgemental. When you embrace both parts within you, you learn to live in harmony with them. When you make peace with both parts of yourself you make peace with the world.

I know a mum who is at war with her two sides. Most of her life she goes about the world being angry; it's as if both sides of her are at war. When you meet her some days she's lovely, smiling and will go to any lengths to help you. Other days she will ignore you in the street and get very argumentative. We all have anger, lust, greed and darkness within us just as we have light, goodness, love and brilliance. We are the world and the world is within us. It's whatever we choose to perceive.

"You choose each experience, you have created it."

CYNIC

The cynic will always survive the soul. The analytical, questioning cynic will see all sides and go deeply into every issue. They will trust less than the soul and will not get sucked into situations based solely (no pun intended) on trust.

I feel the soul will always be threatened by what they perceive as the standoffishness of the cynic. But they shouldn't be.

Some people just can't send out unedited and abundant love to everyone. It doesn't mean that they are unloving; it just means they operate a rationing system on abundant love.

"The cynic and the soul will always survive each other."

5. CAN APPEARANCES BE DECEPTIVE?

SOUL

People judge far too much on appearances and yes, they can be deceiving. I learnt a great lesson about appearances in July 2002. I was preparing to go to the National Speakers Convention in America. It was ten days away and I was getting really hung up about what clothes I was going to wear and how my hair looked, that I had lost touch with my soul and what really matters. It was July 3rd, a beautiful evening, and my daughter and I went for a bike ride. We decided to go to the next village, which had a marina, and ride the bikes around the lake. As we rode along chatting away, suddenly, for no reason, my daughter cut across in front of my bike and I flew over the handle bars and went smash on the pavement. My face was badly cut and the ambulance had to be called. As I was waiting for the ambulance I remember thinking what lesson had I to learn from this accident. A week later while I sat in meditation one morning, I could hear that quiet inner voice speak: "It's not your outer radiance that matters but your inner radiance because when you glow from the inside, the outside glows as well."

"We live in a world where all we see is the tip of an iceberg."

CYNIC

Appearances can be deceiving. I learnt a long time ago to always go beneath the surface and see the real person. I worked for some time in fundraising and one of the greatest lessons I learnt was not to judge people by appearances. The shabbiest person could turn out to be the biggest donor. The people with the flashiest cars and the biggest houses could be the meanest. Everything was on lease and their lavish lifestyle was wildly exceeding their income. You would expect them to be your greatest donors but in fact they were unable or unwilling to give anything.

Sometimes the very things that might impact on you and make you feel uneasy, like great wealth, total self-assurance, and success can be projections and not reality. So it's important not to pay too much attention to the outward appearance.

"Appearances will not deceive if you go behind them."

6. What are the Three Steps to Being a Cynic or a Soul?

Soul

The first step is to learn to let go of being judgemental. Too many people live their lives judging others instead of letting go and judging themselves. When you judge other people you are really only mirroring yourself. If you are honest, what you most dislike in other people is what you most dislike within yourself. Being judgemental can be a waste of energy. If you need to judge, why not judge your own life and let others live their lives.

The second step to being a soul is to learn to love unconditionally. Let go of the attachment of love and the expectations. Unconditional love is all about being there for another human being, no matter what. Unconditional love transmutes all hatred, jealousy, envy, criticism and greed.

The third step to being a soul is that you listen to the inner guidance given to you; you don't need other people's praise or approval all the time. Listen listen, listen and then you cannot fail to hear that still, small voice within you. When you listen to the still, small voice, you will begin to live in harmony with life and your consciousness will expand.

"Live from your soul and remember why you are here."

CYNIC

The first step is to realise the value of having a questioning approach to life. Today we are being asked to accept many things at face value. We are told who the enemy is, whom we should value, who we should listen to. The media is increasingly serving itself rather than the reader or viewer. I recommend that you question everything you are told and make up your own mind. Work on developing your questioning skills.

The second step is to think for yourself. It is all very well to keep up with current events in the world but only if, after you have taken it in, you then think for yourself. How often do you hear people passing on half truths and undigested information. Remember your own values and principles and think your own thoughts. Just because the television tells you something is happening does not mean it's completely true.

The third step is to inform yourself of all the necessary information and then trust your own judgement. You get the necessary information by asking questions, lots of questions. Cultivate your curiosity. I liked this quote by the American poet E.E. Cummings.

> "Once we believe in ourselves, we can risk curiosity, wonder, spontaneous delight, or any experience that reveals the human spirit."

You can transform your life by being constantly curious.

Read widely and query everything you read.

"Be a curious person, question everything."

7. CAN YOU TAKE YOURSELF TOO SERIOUSLY? CAN YOU OVERDO IT?

SOUL

Yes, I believe some people can take the soul too seriously. In life we walk a very fine line between being balanced and unbalanced. We are souls having a human experience and sometimes our ego encourages us to make everything a drama. Good actors play a role and very often have to take that role quite seriously. The true soul does not need to play roles. Yes, the soul can be serious or fun, it just is. When we take ourselves too seriously, it is really our ego looking for attention again. Our true soul does not need to draw attention to itself; it wears no masks and plays no games.

When you find yourself taking yourself too seriously, why not use the following affirmations:

- I have a body but I am not my body.
- I play many roles but you are not your roles.
- I am soul, I am peace.

"It takes a deep commitment to change. It takes an even greater commitment to grow."

CYNIC

Yes, you can take yourself far too seriously and become quite a boring person. In Ireland we talk about having 'craic' which means having a good time. We also talk about 'taking the mick out of someone' which means teasing someone. Traditionally, people who take themselves very seriously are given a hard time in Ireland as humour is always very near the surface.

There is a time and place for seriousness but I find people will often listen more when you appeal to their sense of humour. There is something a little alienating about a person who takes themselves so seriously that they can't laugh at themselves. Think about Alan Alda's words:

> "Laugh at yourself, but don't ever aim your
> doubt at yourself. Be bold."

My advise is to look for the funny side to everything. Practise making a cartoon out of situations and look for the absurd. That will stop you taking yourself too seriously.

"Stop thinking others will take you as seriously as you take yourself."

8. WHAT ARE THE STRENGTHS OF BOTH?

SOUL

The strengths of the soul are that it is eternal and imperishable and its true nature is peace. The soul is a point of light, pure and full of energy and love. The soul sees past illusions and sees what truly is. The soul vibrates at a high resonance and is non-judgemental. To the soul we are all one, we are all interconnected on this great planet called earth. The soul does not know hate, only love. Soul connects us to the world and our purpose here. It introduces us to mystery and helps us reveal the possibilities of our lives.

The strengths of the cynic are its ability to plan and source information. The cynic never misses detail and has an excellent questioning approach. The cynic sees problems and looks for ways to overcome them. The cynic lives in the head and has the ability to see life as a black and white canvas.

I believe the cynic and the soul live in each and everyone of us and we need both to survive and thrive in this 21st century.

"With each and everyone of us there is
something more waiting to be born."

CYNIC

The cynic will always question. Nothing will be accepted at face value. This ensures a thoughtful approach. The cynic will encourage everyone to think for themselves and not to be influenced by accepted norms or prevailing opinion. The cynic will always respect your right to work things out for yourself.

The soul has a firm belief in the goodness of people. This is a wonderful quality which shines through and affects other people. This approach has an energy and a force to it. It inspires people. However, I feel it can also have a naivety to it and can fail to look beneath the surface to people's ulterior motives.

"Always think for yourself. Don't blindly
accept what other people tell you."

9. SOUL/CYNIC INDEX (CONTINUUM)

As we near the end of our conversation, we are in effect like opposite sides of the same coin. We started off thinking that we were polar opposites but have gradually come to see that we have more in common than we thought. We realised that in fact we occupy positions on a continuum. It looks like this:

CONTINUUM BETWEEN CYNIC AND SOUL

EXTREME CYNIC			CENTRE POINT			EXTREME SOUL
Extreme cynicism and questioning approach	Always takes a cynic view but sometimes accepts a trusting soul approach	Sees both sides but will be biased to a cynic view	**Balance** between cynic and soul. Seeing both sides to every issue	Sees both sides but will be biased to a soul view	Always takes a soul view but sometimes accepts a cynic's view	**Extreme** soul and blind faith approach

We feel that our fundamental approach comes from the deep conviction of each end of the continuum but that the ideal place would be at or near the middle where we could use the strengths of each side equally.

10. HOW CAN YOU BE BOTH A CYNIC AND A SOUL?

SOUL

I feel that both live within us every day of our lives. I have moments and days in my life when I feel at one with nature and the universe. My thoughts are pure and I am at peace. Then I have other days and moments when my ego takes over and the cynic in me becomes judgemental and too anal. I look for perfection in things then I self sabotage. We need both in our lives; it's called balance.

When we generate our own feelings of contentment, love and self- acceptance, we become free of any dependency on external sources and substances for feelings of contentment and calm. The cynic in us all can be our friend. When we need greater understanding of something in our lives it will encourage us to ask deeper questions and get the proof that something is worth pursuing.

"When you become an observer in your life
you are attuned to the infinite."

CYNIC

You can delve into your soul and follow its directions. You can meditate and listen to your soul speaking. With intention and practice. We can all do that. However, to achieve balance between cynic and soul I would then recommend that you stand back and think. Never do anything blindly.

Always question. This does not put you into conflict with your soul, it refines and strengthens your soul. When Molly has a 'knowing' I always encourage her to apply the 'cynic' approach to it. If it's a sound 'knowing' it will withstand a robust questioning and be the better for it. You can always meditate again on the newly defined idea.

"A combination of soulful 'knowing' and cynic questioning can produce wonderful insights."

11. WILL THE 21ST CENTURY BE THE CENTURY OF THE CYNIC OR THE SOUL?

SOUL

This is the century where both are vibrantly alive. However, people are tired and stressed and many are seeking more meaning to their lives. Whatever we think, our reality affects our intentions, which affects how we think and act, which changes reality. The 21st century is an exciting time to live. As Duane Elgin says, 'We are now living at a time when humanities perceptual paradgon is undergoing one of its rare shifts and that shift has the potential to dramatically transform life for each of us. This shift therefore goes to the core of our lives. It is much more than a change in ideas and how we think. It is a change in our view of reality, identity, social relationships and human purpose.'

Again I stress that we are walking between two worlds – the cynic and the soul and it is an amazing time to live.

"We are living in such exciting times. Bring your light to wherever you show up."

CYNIC

People in the 21st century need to know how to think for themselves. They need to realise that not only should they question everything they are told but they have an obligation to do so. The emergence of power blocks which want you to conform to one way of thinking continues. It does not really matter whether you look East or West, most governments want you to think their way. Many leaders draw power from the supposed rightness of their position. This can be defined by the enemy they have decided to fight. Many leaders inflate the dangers from other countries, faiths or peoples in order to control our thinking. They encourage us to feel that there is an enemy out there, so if you think like us we will protect you.

Never before has a cynical questioning approach been needed more. Don't believe what governments or leaders tell you as absolute truth. Satisfy yourself about it first.

"Think for yourself now and always."

5 Steps To Symbiosis Or Sabotage

Soul

1. Take time each day to exercise and meditate.

2. Practise the art of discipline. What areas of your
   life right now could be more disciplined?

3. You become what you think about all day long – are
   you becoming what you want to become?

4. Let go of being judgemental – it drains your life force.

5. Live lightly, have fun along the way and
   don't take yourself too seriously.

Cynic

1. Use your energy wisely. Don't waste it on pointless activity.

2. Always go behind appearances.

3. Be a curious person. Question everything.

4. Don't take yourself too seriously.

5. Think for yourself. Don't accept what others
   tell you. Work things out for yourself.

ARE YOU A CYNIC OR A SOUL

THE QUESTIONS	CYNIC	SOUL
1. How do cynics/souls manage their energy?		
2. How can the soul survive in the cynic's world		
3. Is the cynic the shadow of the soul?		
4. Can one survive the other?		
5. Can appearances be deceptive?		
6. What are the three steps to being a cynic or a soul?		
7. Can you take yourself too seriously? Can you overdo it?		
8. What are strengths of both?		
9. Soul/cynic index (continuum)		
10. How can you be both a cynic and a soul?		
11. Will the 21st century be the century of the cynic or the soul?		
SUBTOTAL		

Printed in the United Kingdom
by Lightning Source UK Ltd.
115639UKS00001B/253-375